# For the Sake of

# HIS NAME

..........................................................

## DAVID M. DORAN

Scripture taken from the NEW AMERICAN STANDARD BIBLE®,
Copyright © 1960, 1962, 1963, 1968, 1971, 1973, 1975, 1977, 1995 by The
Lockman Foundation. *Used by permission.*
ISBN-13: 9781980303268

*To the Lord of the Harvest*

# CONTENTS

# FOREWORD

As Christians we are to live in obedience to our Lord's parting words: "All authority in heaven and on earth has been given to me. Go therefore and make disciples of all nations, baptizing them in the name of the Father and of the Son and of the Holy Spirit, teaching them to observe all that I have commanded you. And behold, I am with you always, to the end of the age" (Matthew 28:18-20) (ESV).

In this book Dr. David Doran, senior pastor of Inter-City Baptist Church and President of Detroit Baptist Theological Seminary, challenges a new generation to carry forward world missions. As a pastor committed to expository preaching, he has a burden to call many to missions out of obedience to Christ and the Scriptures.

Last year I met Dr. Doran and found that we shared a common commitment to advance the gospel of our Lord, Jesus Christ. We both have established mission sending agencies in our respective churches in order to most effectively engage in international ministry. We share an understanding that each generation needs to hear the biblical call to take up the mantle of world missions.

Dr. Doran has written a collection of insightful, biblically-informed articles on the topic of missions. They write to students interested in missions, yet pastors and church leaders would also benefit from the breadth of topics and depth of their treatment. These men organized a series of mission conferences for students beginning with Mission 2000 and then founded Student Global Impact. Against this background, the first chapters offer a historical critique of the Student Volunteer Movement. The following chapters address the supremacy of God in missions and then examine the Great Commission in depth. The final chapters survey practical issues such as the role of the local church, the call to missions, and living as a "global" student.

As you read this book, my prayer is that the supremacy of Christ and the power of His gospel will stir your heart and, like Dr. Doran, you will call the next generation to world missions.

# PREFACE

This book is a revised and abridged edition of an earlier work under the same title. The original was written for a student missions conference and was designed to help shed some historical and theological light on the Student Volunteer Movement as well as lay out a pastoral theology of missions. The original book is no longer available, and I have received regular requests for another printing of it. In the years since the first edition, some changes in the authors' ministry focus and location makes it unwise to republish the book as it was originally written. In place of the full work, I have decided to make my chapters from the earlier format of the book available to help churches and pastors. And I've added one additional chapter, an adapted version of a journal article on how the doctrine of the sovereignty of God empowers missions.

I had hoped to do a complete rewrite of my sections of the book before making them available again, but I have not squeezed out the time to do so, and I've also been burdened to develop a different type of book to aid local churches in developing a Great Commission mindset. I am in the midst of working on that project (tentative working title is A Church Member's Guide to Missions). A few missions conference invitations in 2016 and 2017 presented me with renewed requests for the material you have before you, so I decided to venture into electronic publishing to meet those requests.

As mentioned above, I had hoped to do a significant revision of the material to update it in light of recent publications, as well as to clarify and strengthen areas which I think could use it. I have surrendered to the reality that it would be better to get the unrevised version out than to wait for something that doesn't look likely to happen very soon (if at all). Perhaps it is appropriate here to quote myself, from the original preface, about the approach taken in this book:

Because this book was written for a very specific group and purpose, the substance and shape of the book reflects this. Rather than serve as a technical work on missions and the history of missions, we have attempted to bridge the gulf between scholarly and popular writing. We hope you find all that we have written to be based on careful study and communicated with accuracy and clarity. Our highest ambition is to honor God through faithfulness to His Word.

There have been a few minor editorial changes in this edition, but nothing changing the substance of its argument. I remain convinced that missions must be God-centered and that means that not only is God's glory our motivation, but His Word is the authoritative source for understanding how to magnify His glory. In other words, God's glory isn't only why we do missions, it determines the what, how, and where of missions too. My prayer is that this version of the book will be used to stir and strengthen local churches so that our hearts burn with zeal for God's glory and we are freshly motivated and equipped to go to the unreached peoples and places of the earth for the sake of His Name!

# For the Sake of

# HIS NAME

DAVID M. DORAN

*For from Him and through Him and to Him are all things.*
*To Him be the glory forever. Amen.*

Romans 11:36

# 1

# THE SUPREMACY OF GOD IN MISSIONS

No idea is more seductive and pernicious than this: It's all about you. Throughout church history, even those who earnestly desired to do the will of God have fallen prey to this lie. They have pastored large churches, pioneered great missions movements, started successful Christian non-profits, all dependent on human strength and human methods, with the ultimate goal of benefiting humans. Each time the results are disastrous. The churches drift into heresy, the missions movements die out or morph into social help groups, and the non-profits fail to proclaim the truths upon which they were founded.

The root of the problem is the same each time: the goal is man-centered, not God-centered. And when God's people focus on man, his needs, his methods, his earthly happiness, their movements will drift away from biblical truth and God's design for ministry.

The Student Volunteer Movement of the late 19th and early 20th centuries provides a powerful reminder of what happens when missions shifts its focus from God to man. The Movement began sincerely. Students at American universities organized an impressive missions effort. But what began with a focus on reaching people with the gospel ended with a handful of non-profits, focused solely on physical needs, such as the YMCA.

When the first edition of this book came out at the beginning of the 21st century, God was stirring the hearts of young people to mobilize for world missions. Countries previously closed were opening up and still other countries beckoned adventurous young people with the prospect of closed-access tent-making. I wrote this book intending to help young people interested in missions form a biblical philosophy of missions, so that they would not drift into the same man-centered thinking of past missions movements. Today the explosion of online content and communication makes it easier than ever to participate in missions, but also to encounter false philosophies and dangerous practices. Forming a solid biblical philosophy of missions activity in the information age is crucial.

Some man-centeredness is subtle and sophisticated, some is overt and pragmatic. Often it is simply a matter of making man's needs the ultimate motivation for missions. Bill Hybels and Mark Mittelberg provide an illustration of this man-centeredness while writing on evangelism. In offering argument for why believers should be concerned about reaching unbelievers, they start by appealing to an "Anthropic Principle."

> So the lesson we can draw from the Anthropic Principle is this: *Someone* must have gone to a lot of effort to make things just right so that you and I could be here to enjoy life. In short, modern science points to the fact that *we must really matter to God*![1]

Although mankind is the pinnacle of God's creative activity, the Scriptures are clear that God created all things for His glory. "All things have been created through Him and for Him" (Col. 1:16). As Paul concludes his profound discussion of God's sovereign purposes in Romans 9-11, he draws our attention to God: "For from Him and through Him and to Him are all things. To Him be the glory forever. Amen" (11:36). God created man for his own glory and pleasure. Therefore, the proper biblical response to the wonder of creation is to stand in awe of God's glory, not gush about how much man matters to God.

So, at the core of any philosophy of missions must be a basic question about its ultimate purpose or goal. Is missions primarily centered on

---

[1] Bill Hybels and Mark Mittelberg, *Becoming A Contagious Christian* (Grand Rapids: Zondervan, 1994), 14.

man or on God? Is missions an ultimate goal or is it a means to an ultimate goal? Without apology, I contend that John Piper is correct when he writes:

> Missions is not the ultimate goal of the church. Worship is. Missions exists because worship doesn't. Worship is ultimate, not missions, because God is ultimate, not man. When this age is over, and the countless millions of the redeemed fall on their faces before the throne of God, missions will be no more. It is a temporary necessity. But worship abides forever.[2]

We must be willing to go against the grain of our man-centered world to ground our obedience to God in the highest motive possible—God's glory. The Scriptures are clear: the ultimate goal and driving force behind our missions activity ought to be God's glory.

## *The Principle of God-Centered Missions*

> "For all things are for your sakes, so that the grace which is spreading to more and more people may cause the giving of thanks to abound to the glory of God" (2 Cor. 4:15).

Second Corinthians 4 is a good starting point for understanding the biblical basis for missions. Paul presents a logical argument in this passage that concludes with the glory of God. In order to understand the argument properly, we must follow the steps Paul takes to get to that conclusion. He has just been discussing his willingness to be "delivered over to death for Jesus' sake" (v. 11) because he ministers from the basis of faith in God's promises, namely that "He who raised the Lord Jesus will raise us also with Jesus" (v. 14). Because of that willingness, he keeps speaking for Christ (v. 13). On this basis, Paul confirms to them that "all things are for your sakes." He willingly sacrifices himself to preach the gospel for the sake of these

---

[2] John Piper, *Let the Nations Be Glad!* (Grand Rapids: Baker, 1993), 11.

Corinthians (and the other Gentiles to whom he was commissioned an apostle).

If Paul stopped there, this passage would seem to contradict my thesis. But Paul's next clause gives us the reason why "all things are for your sakes." The words translated "so that" are a *hina* clause in Greek that reveal purpose. The first part of the verse deals with *what* Paul does (sacrifices himself in ministering to the Gentiles), but the second part of the verse tells *why* Paul does it.

Paul's ultimate purpose is communicated in very complicated grammar, but the basic thrust is clear: the increase of grace makes for an increase of thanksgiving to the glory of God. Whether that grace is grace working in Paul (so that he can suffer and speak; KJV) or through Paul so that more and more people receive it (NASB, NIV), is a point of debate. The bottom line, however, is not a point of debate—the ultimate goal and driving purpose of his missionary work is God's glory!

This text also helps us provide balance to our missions mindset. We have no excuse to use a God-centered purpose to develop a missions strategy that is out of balance with biblical truth.

Two balancing implications may be drawn from these words:

*This does not mean that no other goals exist.* The very fact that Paul states "all things are for your sakes" (lit. "on account of you") means reaching and ministering to the Corinthians was one of his "goals." He is even more clear in 1 Corinthians 9:19, "For though I am free from all men, I have made myself a slave to all, so that I may win more." Paul clearly aimed to win men and women to Jesus Christ. He even went to great lengths to not offend the people he aimed to reach by adopting their practices in non-moral matters.

> To the weak I became weak, that I might win the weak; I have become all things to all men, so that I may by all means save some (1 Cor. 9:22).

Just as I also please all men in all things, not seeking my own profit but the profit of the many, so that they may be saved (1 Cor. 10:33).

*This does not mean that all other goals are unimportant.* Paul demonstrates the importance of reaching people for Christ in the words "the grace which is spreading to more and more people." The point of this text is that when the gospel spreads to more and more people, more and more thanksgiving abounds to the glory of God.

Our God-centered commitment should not reduce our desire to see sinners saved from sin and condemnation; it should heighten it! The chief means by which God will glorify Himself, if you accept the weight given in Scripture, is by saving people "from every tribe and tongue and people and nation" (Rev. 5:9). God is glorified both in the salvation of sinners and the condemnation of sinners (Rev. 19:1-6)—but salvation is the chief means He uses to accomplish His glory. Scripture focuses on redemption, not condemnation. The Lamb is worthy because He has redeemed us!

How do we balance the supposed tension between seeking God's glory and man's salvation? My point is to argue that we can only have one ultimate goal—and that goal must be God-centered. God's glory rules the pursuit of all other goals. The pursuit of God's glory is the only pursuit large enough to control all others and to encompass all others into itself. If God's glory comes first, then there are some things that cannot be done in our efforts to win souls for Jesus Christ. A God-centered focus is the only one that is large enough to encompass all that God calls on us to do—it scoops up and embraces all that God has commanded of us, whether on the mission fields of the world or on the home front.

## The Proof of God-Centered Missions

While 1 Corinthians 4:15 provides adequate grounding for God-centered missions, looking at the larger context helps us understand how the goal of God's glory perfectly fits the missions endeavor. When missions is successful and people turn in faith to Christ, God receives glory in several specific ways. Let us examine how Paul uses the language and concept of glory in the first several chapters of 2 Corinthians.

### *Our Response to the Gospel Acknowledges God's Glory*

For as many as are the promises of God, in Him they are yes; therefore also through Him is our Amen to the glory of God through us (2 Cor. 1:20).

In a context where it appears that the Corinthians were questioning Paul's honesty, he defends himself and his gospel as being true; that neither he nor the gospel are contradicting themselves by saying "yes" and "no" at the same time. The promises of God are all certain and guaranteed in Jesus Christ, and the believer is the one who has said Amen to those promises. We give our "Amen" back to God through Jesus Christ for the glory of God.

In other words, to believe God's promises (i.e., say Amen to them) is to give God glory, to honor Him. To doubt or deny God's promises (i.e., not say Amen to them) is to dishonor God. This is exactly what Jesus meant when He confronted the Pharisees of His day:

> So that all will honor the Son even as they honor the Father. He who does not honor the Son does not honor the Father who sent Him. Truly, truly, I say to you, he who hears My word, and believes Him who sent Me, has eternal life, and does not come into judgment, but has passed out of death into life (John 5:23-24).

Based on the divine commentary regarding Abraham's faith, it is safe to conclude that faith is an essential requirement for glorifying God:

> Without becoming weak in faith he contemplated his own body, now as good as dead since he was about a hundred years old, and the deadness of Sarah's womb; yet, with respect to the promise of God, he did not waver in unbelief but grew strong in faith, giving glory to God, and being fully

assured that what God had promised, He was able also to perform (Rom. 4:19-21).

Hebrews 11:6 also states the matter quite clearly:

> And without faith it is impossible to please Him, for he who comes to God must believe that He is and that He is a rewarder of those who seek Him.

That God receives glory when people respond to the gospel in faith proves the doxological focus of missions.

### *The Believer's Transformation Reflects God's Glory*

The third time we encounter the idea of glory and 2 Corinthians is when Paul discusses the believer's transformation into the Lord's image, a transformation that is described as moving from glory to glory by the Spirit's work.

> But we all, with unveiled face, beholding as in a mirror the glory of the Lord, are being transformed into the same image from glory to glory, just as from the Lord, the Spirit (2 Cor. 3:18).

This transformation takes place as we behold the Lord's glory in the Word. At first glance one might question how this relates to the task of missions, but I believe the answer is not far from us if we think theologically about God's purpose in saving us. God saves people for the purpose of displaying His glory in those who are saved. That glory is the restoration of God's image in man, or, viewed in relation to Jesus Christ, the transformation of the redeemed into His image. Consider the pattern Scripture sets forth.

### God's Original Design: Man, as God's Image and Glory

God created man to serve as His representative over creation. The Bible teaches that mankind, as the pinnacle of God's creative work, was made in the image of God. 1 Corinthians 11:7 says, "For a man ought not to have his head covered, since he is the image and glory of God; but the woman is the glory of man." There is debate about

7

the exact nature of the image of God in man, but the text clearly affirms that man, as a finite replica of the infinite God, was created to reflect the glory of his Creator.

## The Result of Sin: God's Image Marred, not Removed

As a result of man's rebellion against God in the Garden, sin entered the world. Romans 3:23 describes that sin in terms of God's glory: "For all have sinned and fall short of the glory of God." Rather than reflect the glory of the Creator, man turned away in disobedience and the consequence was disastrous. Yet, sin did not destroy the image of God in man. After the Fall, God commanded Noah that "whoever sheds man's blood, by man his blood shall be shed, for in the image of God He made man" (Gen. 9:6). The New Testament confirms the image of God in man, warning us of the hypocrisy of blessing God and cursing men who are made in the "likeness of God" (James 3:9). No matter how degraded man may become in this life, he still retains some vestige of God's image.

## The New Birth: God's Image Renewed within the Believer

An amazing element of God's saving grace is that the new birth actually begins the process of re-creation into a perfect reflection of God's image. In telling the Ephesian believers that they should not live like lost people, Paul calls them to "put on the new self, which in the likeness of God has been created in righteousness and holiness of the truth" (Eph. 4:24). Notice how he describes the new birth: "in the likeness of God has been created." And this is not an isolated concept. Colossians 3:10 informs us that believers "have put on the new self who is being renewed to a true knowledge according to the image of the One who created him." In both texts Paul uses the same Greek preposition (*kata*) to indicate that the work of renewal is done according to the pattern of God's image.[3] We have been and are being made into the image of God.

---

[3] Peter T. O'Brien, *The Letter to the Ephesians* (Grand Rapids: Eerdmans, 1999), 332; Murray J. Harris, *Colossians and Philemon* (Grand Rapids: Eerdmans, 1991), 153.

## Final Salvation: Conformed to the Son's Image, the Perfect Representation of God's Image

Not surprisingly then, the Scriptures reveal that God's eternal plan in salvation is to conform the redeemed into the image of His Son, "For those whom He foreknew, He also predestined to become conformed to the image of His Son, so that He would be the firstborn among many brethren" (Rom. 8:29). Jesus Christ is "the radiance of His glory and the exact representation of His nature" (Heb. 1:3), so conformity to Christ is the perfect reflection of God's image. The great hope for all believers is that "when He appears, we will be like Him, because we will see Him just as He is" (1 John 3:2). The grand plan of God's redemption is displaying His glory in those who have been made like His Son. To view salvation as merely a change of destination (heaven vs. hell) is to miss all the grandeur of God's design. He saved us to make us like His Son, which means He saved us to reflect His glory.

## Progressive Sanctification: Changed into Christlikeness by the Spirit through the Word

Now we circle back to 2 Corinthians 3:18. To understand the passage properly, we must consider it in light of God's plan for man's salvation—those whom He saves He will make like Jesus Christ. But that is not the entire biblical picture. Not only *will* God make us like Christ, He *is* making us like Christ through the Word and the work of the Spirit. Paul tells the Corinthians, "But we all, with unveiled face, beholding as in a mirror the glory of the Lord, *are being transformed into the same image from glory to glory*, just as from the Lord, the Spirit." God's sanctifying work right now is progressively transforming believers into the image of Jesus Christ, from glory to glory. God is not content to wait until heaven to make us like Christ. He is actively transforming us now as we look into the Word and behold the glory of Christ (cf. 2 Cor. 4:4-6).

God's purpose in saving sinners is not simply to change their eternal abiding place; it is to change them into the image of His Son so that they reflect His glory. His eternal plan of redemption results in His glory, displayed in the transformed lives of believers, confirming again the doxological purpose of missions.

9

## The Spirit's Work Through the Gospel Displays God's Glory

Growing out of Paul's unapologetic confession that he is not sufficient for the task he has been given (2:14-17), but that God is sufficient (3:5-6), Paul reveals where his hope of "success" in the gospel ministry lies—the power and work of the Holy Spirit (3:7-11). The chief term that Paul uses to contrast the ministry of the law and that of the Spirit is glory. (The Greek word *doxa* is used eight times in 5 verses; *doxazo* is used twice.)

Central to this passage is the statement of v. 8, "how will the ministry of the Spirit fail to be even more with glory?" How is the ministry of the Spirit more glorious than the old covenant? Because it has the power to give life to those under its ministry, and that life-giving power is God's power—so God receives the glory.

The work of missions can only be accomplished by the Spirit's power. And the display of that power brings glory to God, confirming again the doxological focus of missions.

## The Center of the Gospel Message is God's Glory

The fourth passage that confirms my argument is perhaps the most central to the issue. In 4:3-6 Paul confronts the reality that many do not accept the gospel message. In context, he is making it clear that this rejection is not due to any flaws in the message or even in the messengers. If unbelievers reject the gospel, it is because Satan has blinded their minds.

But the passage does not simply state that Satan blinds unbelievers from seeing the gospel. Verse 4 says that Satan "has blinded the minds of the unbelieving so that they might not see the light of the gospel of the *glory of Christ,* who is the image of God." So, the devil keeps people trapped in condemnation by blocking their vision of the "glory of Christ, who is the image of God." The heart of the gospel message, therefore, is the glory of Christ. Verse 6 further expands on God's glory in the gospel by describing the gospel message as "the knowledge of the glory of God in the face of Christ." The gospel that saves people is a gospel that reveals God's glory in Jesus Christ. If people don't accept the gospel, it is because they don't see God's glory in it.

The verse that comes between these two phrases further reinforces this truth. It is precisely because the gospel is "the gospel of the glory of Christ" and "the knowledge of the glory of God in the face of Christ" that Paul without hesitation claims, "we do not preach ourselves but Christ Jesus as Lord." Contrary to many contemporary approaches of evangelism that tailor-make the gospel to fit the needs of the hearer, the biblical gospel focuses first on Christ, not the sinner. We preach Christ, not an eternal life insurance policy or keys to changing your life.

The gospel, the message that is the heart of missions, is the truth that God's glory is revealed in Jesus Christ. He is Lord before whom all will bow, either now in repentance or later in judgment.

### The Believer's Hope in the Gospel Focuses on God's Glory

The fifth passage moves us past our base text. In 4:17-18 Paul begins to highlight the hope of every believer—that God has promised a glory that will outshine anything that this world has to offer. This world is temporal and filled with affliction for Christ's disciples, but these afflictions are light and momentary compared to the far more exceeding and eternal weight of glory that will be revealed. The believer has embraced by faith the promise of this glory, which is God's, and lives "look[ing] not at the things which are seen, but at the things which are not seen; for the things which are seen are temporal, but the things which are not seen are eternal." Or, as Paul will say a few verses later, "we walk by faith, not by sight" (5:7).

The promise of glory with God in eternity is an essential element of the gospel message. Consider the following passages:

• Through whom also we have obtained our introduction by faith into this grace in which we stand; and we exult in hope of the *glory of God*. (Rom. 5:2).

11

- For I consider that the sufferings of this present time are not worthy to be compared with the *glory that is to be revealed to us* (Rom. 8:18).
- That the creation itself also will be set free from its slavery to corruption into the freedom of the *glory of the children of God* (Rom. 8:21).
- And He did so to make known the *riches of His glory upon vessels of mercy, which He prepared beforehand for glory* (Rom. 9:23).
- For our citizenship is in heaven, from which also we eagerly wait for a Savior, the Lord Jesus Christ; who will transform the body of our humble state into conformity with the *body of His glory*, by the exertion of the power that He has even to subject all things to Himself (Phil. 3:20-21).
- When Christ, who is our life, is revealed, then you also will be revealed with Him *in glory* (Col. 3:4).
- So that *the name of our Lord Jesus will be glorified in you*, and you in Him, according to the grace of our God and the Lord Jesus Christ (2 Thess. 1:12).

## *The Practical Implications of God-Centered Missions*

The remainder of this book will develop and elaborate the implications of giving God first place in missions, but it is fitting here to highlight the ones that form the foundational thinking and purpose of this book.

### *The Priority of Missions Must Be Faithfulness to God and His Word, Not Fruitfulness*

Since we can only have one ultimate priority, we must prioritize faithfulness above fruitfulness. This does not mean that we do not want fruitfulness, but that we prize faithfulness to God as more important so that we never pursue fruitfulness at the expense of faithfulness. This was Paul's mindset in 2 Corinthians 2:17, "For we are not like many, peddling the word of God, but as from sincerity, but as from God, we speak in Christ in the sight of God." Being faithful to God's Word means we will never treat it like a commodity to be shaped and molded by marketing strategies, either at home or on a mission field.

Paul again affirms his commitment to faithfulness over fruitfulness in 2 Corinthians 4:2, "but we have renounced the things hidden because of shame, not walking in craftiness or adulterating the word of God, but by the manifestation of truth commending ourselves to every man's conscience in the sight of God." Paul honestly and accurately proclaimed the truth, never distorting it by catering to the whims of the target audience under the guise of what is today being called contextualization. He understood that people do not reject the gospel because of any flaw or deficiency in the message, but because "the god of this world has blinded the minds of the unbelieving" (v. 4). The only antidote to such blindness is the pure gospel message! Distorting the gospel is to give up all hope of seeing lost people saved.

Scripture does not set faithfulness and fruitfulness against each other, but it does place priority on faithfulness. "It is required of stewards that a man be found faithful" (1 Cor. 4:2). Fruitfulness should, and does, grow out of faithfulness, "If you abide in Me, and My words abide in you, ask whatever you wish, and it will be done for you. My Father is glorified by this, that you bear much fruit, and so prove to be My disciples" (John 15:7-8). Abiding precedes fruit-bearing!

### *The Promotion of the Missions Must Be Primarily Based on God and His Glory, Not Man's Needs*

Paul's driving passion was God's glory revealed in Jesus Christ. And he delighted in the day he would stand before Christ, presenting those he had won in an offering of thanks and worship, people who would also give thanks to God for his grace. This God-focused hope propelled Paul's missions efforts. Consider some other texts where Paul describes his motivations:

•       To be a minister of Christ Jesus to the Gentiles, ministering as a priest the gospel of God, so that my offering of the

13

Gentiles may become acceptable, sanctified by the Holy Spirit (Rom. 15:16).

- For who is our hope or joy or crown of exultation? Is it not even you, in the presence of our Lord Jesus at His coming (1 Thess. 2:19)?
- For I am jealous for you with a godly jealousy; for I betrothed you to one husband, so that to Christ I might present you as a pure virgin (2 Cor. 11:2)
- Now while Paul was waiting for them at Athens, his spirit was being provoked within him as he was observing the city full of idols (Acts 17:16).
- And saying, "Men, why are you doing these things? We are also men of the same nature as you, and preach the gospel to you that you should turn from these vain things to a living God, *who made the heaven and the earth and the sea and all that is in them* (Acts 14:15).
- For they themselves report about us what kind of a reception we had with you, and how you turned to God from idols to serve a living and true God (1 Thess. 1:9).

In each of these texts Paul's focus is seeing God exalted and worshiped as the One who alone is worthy to be called God and to receive all worship. Mankind has deep needs that matter for all of eternity, but unless we give God precedence over all human needs, we risk weakening our efforts to meet those needs.

This God-centered perspective, versus the man-centered one, is a fundamental requirement of pleasing God *and* benefiting people. "If the pursuit of *God's* glory is not ordered above the pursuit of *man's* good in the affections of the heart and the priorities of the church, *man* will not be well served and *God* will not be duly honored."[4] When we adopt a man-centered approach—as is very common in modern missions practice—we go counter to its ultimate goal. The pursuit of man's perceived needs is at the core of man's flight from God, and it is poor handling of Scripture to cast God in the role of Cosmic Need-Meeter. The driving force of redemption is not meeting needs—it is to magnify God's grace (Eph. 2:7). "God's first love is

---

[4] John Piper, *Let the Nations Be Glad!*, 12.

rooted in the value of his holy name, not the value of sinful people. And because it is, there is hope for sinful people—since they are not the ground of their salvation, God's name is."[5]

Jonathan Edwards made this same argument in his day:

> Here God acting for *himself,* or making himself his last end, and his acting for *their* sake, are not to be set in opposition; they are rather to be considered as coinciding one with the other, and implied one in the other. But yet God is to be considered first and original in his regard; and the creature is the object of God's regard, consequently, and by implication, as being as it were comprehended in God.[6]

We must return to the God-centered vision of the Scriptures if we hope to stir God's people deeply to pursue the cause of world missions with all of the potential suffering and sacrifices that entails. We should have great compassion for the needs of people, but we must have a greater passion for the glory of God.

### The Practice of Missions Must Be Controlled by Scripture, Not Traditions or Trends

In 2 Corinthians 2:16, Paul made it abundantly clear that he lacked any sense of fleshly self-confidence when he asked the question, "And who is adequate for these things?" The question assumes a negative answer. As Paul declared man's insufficiency, he implied the manner in which we practice missions is subject to God's authority in the Word. The standard for what we do is not what we have always done (tradition) or what everybody is doing right now (trends); it must be the unchanging Word of God.

This is not to suggest that there is no flexibility in the ministry applications we make on the various mission fields of the world. But there is no flexibility on the biblical principles that are to be applied.

---

[5] John Piper, *The Pleasures of God* (Portland: Multnomah Press, 1991), 108.

[6] *Dissertation on the End for Which God Created the World,* in *The Works of Jonathan Edwards,* 2 vols., rev. and ed. Edward Hickman (Carlisle, PA: Banner of Truth Trust, 1974), 1:101.

The arguments, "it has always been done this way" and "this is how everyone does it," should not satisfy us nor stand against Scripture.

We have allowed many traditional practices to become entrenched to the point that we act as if they are biblical. No one likes raising questions about the way well-intentioned, godly people have and are serving the Lord, but we must have a higher allegiance to God than to people. In light of the missionary challenges that confront us at the start of the twenty-first century, I believe we should be fully prepared to evaluate what we are doing by God's Word so that we can move forward with confidence that we are obeying Him, not the false confidence that we can do it better than He instructed us.

### *The Power for Missions Must be Divine, Not Human*

We have seen that Paul expected the work of missions to be conducted in the power of the Spirit, and that His power would be a display of God's glory (2 Cor. 3:7-11). I believe that a subtle evidence of our man-centeredness is our dependence upon our plans, programs, and preparation. Giving God first place in the missions endeavor also means that we consciously commit ourselves to simple planning and fervent praying. Intricately orchestrated programs that reflect our ingenuity also tend to deflate our humility and inflate our sense of sufficiency. The biblical bottom line is that we are not sufficient for the task, but God is! He has given us the Spirit and the Word, and those gifts must remain the central focus of all missionary planning and practice because they are the only source of missionary power.

I am obviously in favor of education and training—it is part of my life and ministry—but these are no substitutes for the Spirit's power. I believe in good organization (even if I do not always practice it!) and effective methods, but these too are no substitute for the more glorious ministry of the Spirit. Is it possible that we have lost sight of a central qualification for ministry and evidence of God's call on a missionary's life—the Spirit's transforming and empowering presence? Is it possible that we talk more about five-year plans and carefully crafted programs than we do the need for God's power through the Spirit upon the ministry of the Word?

In 1715, Louis XIV of France died. This king had called himself "the Great" and had proudly boasted, "I am the State!" During his time, his court was the most magnificent in Europe. His funeral, too, was designed to be a display of his greatness—and it was spectacular. His body laid in a golden coffin. To amplify the deceased king's grandeur by drawing attention solely to him, the orders had been given to light the cathedral very dimly, and to set one special candle above his coffin. The massive crowd gathered for the funeral waited in silence. Then Massillon, who later became Bishop of Clermont, slowly reaching down, snuffed out the candle and said, "Only God is great!" Louis XIV came and went, but the spirit that energized him is still at work in this world. Billions are lost in darkness, blinded by the god of this world so that they do not see God's glory in the face of Jesus Christ.

Unless we revive our commitment to the principle that God alone is great, we will not rise to the challenges of missions in the twenty-first century. Unless our souls burn within us with holy jealousy at the sight of false worship and with an all-consuming passion to see Christ exalted, we will not pay the price that biblical missions demands. As I first wrote this book at the start of the 21st century, the President of the United States had called this country to defend itself against the terrorist attacks of September 11, 2001. Thousands of military personnel were being deployed to the other side of the globe, and millions more back home were firmly committed to back them in their task. I believed the cause was right, but I was troubled by the fact that many American Christians who would not hesitate to send their sons into battle for the American way of life, did hesitate to consider sending them to the mission fields of the world. The Lord of lords has called us to take His name to the ends of the earth, and if He is supreme in our lives, we will heed His call. We will go, we will send, we will give, and we will pray, all *For the Sake of His Name.*

*We proclaim Him, admonishing every man and teaching every man with all wisdom, so that we may present every man complete in Christ.*

Colossians 1:28

# 2

# THE TASK OF THE GREAT COMMISSION I: THE MEANING OF DISCIPLESHIP

The goal of the last chapter was to demonstrate that missions must be God-centered, not man-centered. Missions is God's "taking from among the Gentiles a people for His name" (Acts 15:14) and our going into the nations "for the sake of the Name" (3 John 7). There can only be one center—it is either man and his needs or it is God and His glory! There can only be one ultimate or final goal, and all other goals must be subordinate to it. Is the saving of souls God's ultimate goal or is it a goal that is subordinate to an ultimate goal? Does the Bible teach that redemption is for the ultimate purpose of man's good or God's glory?

Based on 2 Corinthians 4:15, I argued that saving souls is a means to an end: God's glory. To take the argument a step further, consider some passages from the book of Ephesians. In chapter 1, Paul summarizes God's redemptive purposes and actions with the words "to the praise of the glory of His grace" (v. 6), "to the praise of His glory" (v. 12), and "to the praise of His glory" (v.14). In Ephesians 2, Paul tells us that God's merciful work of making us alive, raising us up, and seating us in the heavenly places is "so that in the ages to come He might show the surpassing riches of His grace in kindness toward us in Christ Jesus" (v. 7). In Ephesians 3, Paul argues that preaching the "unfathomable riches of Christ" to the Gentiles was "so that the manifold wisdom of God might now be made known through the church to the rulers and the authorities in the heavenly places" (v. 10). All three of these passages clearly indicate that the ultimate goal is God's glory. God provided salvation for the praise of the glory of His grace. He offers salvation as a gift of grace so that man will praise Him for His kindness and not boast of their self-efforts. And he graciously includes Gentiles in his plan of redemption to display his divine wisdom.

That God's glory is the end goal of missions does not diminish the importance of either the provision or proclamation of salvation; it puts them in their proper place—ends by which God is glorifying Himself. Since He pursues His own glory with intense passion, His provision of salvation is rich and bountiful, and our proclamation of salvation carries His promise of power and effectiveness. The goals of God's glory and man's good are not at odds with each other. John MacArthur correlates the two factors well:

> The supreme way in which God chose to glorify Himself was through the redemption of sinful men, and it is through participation in that redemptive plan that believers themselves most glorify God.... Therefore the believer who desires to glorify God, who wants to honor God's supreme will and purpose, must share God's love for the lost world and share in His mission to redeem the lost to Himself. Christ came into the world that He loved and sought to win sinners to Himself for the Father's glory. As Christ's representatives, we are likewise sent into the world that He loves to bring the lost to Him and thereby bring glory and honor to God. Our mission is the same as that of the Father and of the Son.[7]

Rather than compete with each other, one (man's good) is subordinate to the other (God's glory). In other words, God glorifies Himself by graciously saving sinners.

From this proper God-centered perspective, we can now move to consider more specifically our responsibility to fulfill the Great Commission. Even though our ultimate goal in missions must be

---

[7] John MacArthur, *Matthew 24-28* (Chicago: Moody, 1989), 331-333.

God's glory, we can never use that mindset to excuse apathy and disobedience. Genuine commitment to God's glory is displayed in obedience to His will. As Christ's disciples, we must imitate the pattern of obedience to the Father that He set for us. The crucial connection between our aim (to glorify God) and our action (obedience to God's will) is found in the Lord's prayer recorded in John 17:4, "I glorified You on the earth, having accomplished the work which You have given Me to do." Note the close connection between God's glory and the Son's obedience: "I have glorified…having accomplished the work." Glorifying the Father was not some abstract concept for Jesus; He glorified his Father by accomplishing His work—a concrete expression of obedience. "Jesus has glorified the Father in that He has finished His assigned task."[8] Earlier in John 4, Jesus claimed, "My food is to do the will of Him who sent Me and to accomplish His work" (v. 34). The Father's will and work were the consuming passion of the Son, and the Son's will and work must be our consuming passion if we really intend to bring Him honor and glory.

It is, therefore, essential that we come to understand clearly what Jesus Christ has commissioned us to do so that we can glorify Him on the earth, accomplishing what He has given us to do. The basis for our study will be the commission statement found in Matthew 28:18-20, but I will seek to correlate the truths found here with those found in the other commission texts and the rest of the New Testament record and commentary on their fulfillment.

## *The Exposition of Christ's Commission*

Since we must draw our view of the missionary task from the biblical text, not impose upon it, we will start with a simple exposition of this crucial passage. In it our Lord sets forth His desire for the church during the interregnum.[9] The Lord Himself established the terminal point for this commission by using the phrase "even to the end of the age" (v. 20). Given the significance of this passage, we will first closely

---

[8] Leon Morris, *The Gospel According to John*, NIC (Grand Rapids: Eerdmans, 1971), 721.

[9] The interregnum is the church age.

examine the text itself, its content and message. We can break down the content into three divisions: the authority for the program of the church (v. 18), the statement of the program (vv. 19-20a), and a word of reassurance about the program (v. 20b).

> When they saw Him, they worshiped Him; but some were doubtful. And Jesus came up and spoke to them, saying, "All authority has been given to Me in heaven and on earth. Go therefore and make disciples of all the nations, baptizing them in the name of the Father and the Son and the Holy Spirit, teaching them to observe all that I commanded you; and lo, I am with you always, even to the end of the age" (Matt. 28:17-20).

### *The Authority for the Program*

The Lord addresses the doubt of some of the disciples with a definitive statement about His person and authority. First, He describes the character of His authority. The authority that Christ possesses is His because He is the Divine Son of God, the Messiah. This has been incontrovertibly proven by His resurrection from the dead (cf. Rom. 1:3-4; Acts 2:25-36). It is also a delegated authority that has been given to Him by the Father. Ephesians 1:20-22 reveals that the authority is granted through the exaltation of Christ to the right hand of the Father. He is exalted above principalities and powers and every name that is named. Philippians 2:9-11 declares that this authority is granted because of His obedience to the will of the Father. Christ is exalted above all, and every knee will bow to Him.

Secondly, Christ explains the comprehensiveness of His authority: "all authority...in heaven and in earth." The point is not merely that Jesus has authority; Matthew is full of displays of Jesus' authority (His words, 24:35; He forgives sin, 9:6; and He casts out demons, 12:22-29). The point is that His authority is universal in scope.[10]

---

[10] D. A. Carson, "Matthew" in *EBC* (Grand Rapids: Zondervan, 1984), 594.

Why is the authority of the Lord so important to the Great Commission? Because the church faces intense spiritual conflict as they obey the Lord's commands. At the very outset of His earthly ministry, with whom did the Lord engage in conflict? Satan (cf. 4:1-11). Throughout His ministry, over whom was He exerting authority? Again, it is Satan (cf. 12:22-29). The Gospel of Matthew reveals that Satan is actively plucking the seed of the Word out of the soil of men's hearts so that they will not come to know the Savior (Matt. 13:19). The New Testament epistles demonstrate that the Church carries on this battle. It is Satan and his forces with whom believers wrestle (Eph. 6:10 ff.), and who seek to hinder the work of the gospel (1 Thess. 2:18). Satan and his wicked host stand defeated by the Jesus the Lord (Col. 2:15), and one day the Lord will crush Satan under the feet of the church (Rom. 16:20). But today the church must actively wage war against Satan's attacks. While we wait for the final defeat of Satan we must remember that the task of making disciples calls us to raid his kingdom of darkness to deliver the god of this world's captives (cf. 2 Cor. 4:4; 2 Tim. 2:26). It would be foolish to think that the church can do this on the basis of its own authority. The church must engage in this conflict on the solid ground of the authority of the Lord of lords and King of kings.

### *The Activity of the Program*

Although we tend to see a number of commands in Matthew 28:19-20, the fact is that the commission as presented here contains one command and a number of participles that fill in additional information about that command. The single imperative, or command of the commission, is found in the words, "make disciples of all nations." The disciples are to do what He did—make disciples. Given the current debates about the meaning of discipleship, we will look at this issue very carefully in the next section of this chapter. Accompanying this single imperative are participles that provide us with insight into the circumstances in which disciple making is to take place and the characteristics of disciple making.

#### The Circumstances of the Program

The first participle of verse 19, translated by the simple word "go" modifies the command to make disciples by detailing the circumstances in which the church is to make disciples. The idea of the Greek grammar is that the disciple making will take place as the church is "going." It is not strictly a command for the church to go, but it speaks of the church's making disciples as a part of its normal operations. Some have tried to argue from this grammatical fact that there is no basis here for going anywhere, only that the church, wherever it is, should be making disciples. This argument, however, mishandles the text.

First, grammatically, "When a participle functions as a circumstantial participle dependent on an imperative, it normally gains some imperatival force."[11] An attendant circumstance participle may be defined as communicating "an action that, in some sense, is coordinate with the finite verb. In this respect it is not dependent, for it is translated like a verb."[12] In other words, "The 'going' was not an incidental matter, as if He was saying, 'whenever you happen to go on a trip, try to make a few disciples wherever you are.'"[13] The Lord was clearly directing them to do something ("go") that had to take place prior to the main command ("make disciples").[14] Secondly, that Christ's followers were commanded to "make disciples of all the nations" certainly means that they would have to go to those nations. In D. A. Carson's words, "it is difficult to believe that 'go' has lost all imperatival force."[15] Thirdly, the other commission passages in Scripture make it absolutely clear that the command extends to the whole world, and that the believers are being sent into it (cf. Acts 1:8; Luke 24:45-49; John 17:18, 20:21).

**The Characteristics of the Program**
There are two more participles used in these verses that supply additional information on the central command of making disciples:

---

[11] Carson, 595.

[12] Daniel B. Wallace, *Greek Grammar Beyond the Basics* (Grand Rapids: Zondervan, 1996), 640.

[13] Steven C. Hawthorne, "Mandate on the Mountain" in *Perspectives on the World Christian Movement*, 3rd ed. (Pasadena: Carey Library, 1999), 110.

[14] Wallace (643) argues that the attendant circumstance participle serves as "something of a prerequisite before the action of the main verb can occur."

[15] Carson, 595.

"baptizing" and "teaching." Their exact relation to the main verb is debated, so dogmatic statement is not possible, but it is probably best to understand them as revealing the characteristics of disciple making. They are not strictly the means by which disciples are made, but rather the marks of disciple making. An example of this use of the participle is found in Luke 6:35, "lend, expecting nothing in return." "Expecting nothing in return" is not technically how the money was lent, but instead it describes the mindset the lender should have.[16]

The first participle or characteristic of disciple making is baptizing, a time when a disciple identifies himself with the Lord and yields himself to the authority of His Teacher. It is a terrible mistake to assume that since baptism is not necessary for salvation, that it is unimportant or even of minor importance. If the Lord commanded the church to make disciples, calling out baptism as a hallmark of the disciple-making process, it is extremely unwise to minimize the importance of this ordinance.

The second characteristic of disciple making is teaching the disciple all the commandments of the Lord. The New Testament does not teach an evangelism that neglects instructing a convert in the truths and teachings of the Master. Modern evangelistic methods that drive for a decision for Christ but fail to instruct disciples are not following the commission given to the church by Jesus Christ.

### *The Assurance During the Program*

The Lord closes the commission with words of assurance for the disciples as they are about to embark on the most dynamic work ever begun: "Lo, I am with you always, even to the end of the age." He promises His divine, continual, and enduring presence. Jesus Christ, the divine, omnipotent Son of God promises to be with His people, bringing with Him all the authority in heaven and on earth (v. 18). And He pledges to be with them "always." The word translated "always" is a unique word that means literally, "the whole of every day." Jesus assures His people that He will be with them, not in just

---

[16] Ibid., 597.

a vague "always" sense, but for each moment of every day. [17] "Days of strength and of weakness, days of success and of failure, of joy and of sorrow, of youth and of age, days of life and day of death—all the days."[18] And this continual presence is enduring, "even to the end of the age"—until the consummation of world history. As the church faces the passing of time, it can rely on the presence of Christ. He will never leave his bride throughout this entire age. As D.A. Carson notes, "The period between commission and consummation is indefinite in length; but whatever its duration, it is the time of the church's mission and of preliminary enjoyment of her Lord's presence."[19]

Not only does the church today have the record of Christ's commission in the New Testament text, we also have the benefit of seeing it lived out through the book of Acts. It is encouraging and fascinating to note how Acts 11:19-26 details the record of the church's faithful execution of the program that the Lord Jesus Christ prescribed. Notice the similarities: 1) they were "going" (vv. 19-20); 2) they were "making disciples" (vv. 21b, 24b); 3) they were "instructing them" (v. 26); and, 4) the "Lord was with them," (v. 21a).

## *The Essence of Christ's Commission*

As we have already noted, the central focus of this passage is the command to make disciples. Anyone who wants to obey Christ seriously must understand what it means to make disciples. This is the essential task of the Great Commission, not simply announcing the good news of Jesus Christ. We cannot make disciples without announcing the good news (Rom. 10:14-17), but that is where the Great Commission starts, not stops.

Perhaps an illustration will make the distinction clearer. Suppose I could somehow harness the marvels of modern technology to orchestrate a satellite broadcast of a gospel message into every nation of the world. Would that fulfill the Great Commission? Let's

---

[17] Ibid., 599.

[18] John A. Broadus, *Matthew* (Valley Forge: Judson Press, 1886), 597.

[19] Carson, "Matthew," 599.

say I could somehow arrange that every person on the globe would actually hear that satellite broadcast. Would it be fulfilled then? Both of these scenarios would be great cause for rejoicing, but my argument, based on the text of Matthew 28:19-20, is that neither would fulfill the Great Commission. They would be the first step in fulfilling it, but the Lord's command demands more than simply preaching the gospel to all the nations, or even to every person in those nations. The Lord commanded us to make disciples of all nations.

Let's sharpen our focus on the essence of the Great Commission by considering two important questions: What does it mean to be a disciple of Jesus Christ? And how are disciples of Jesus Christ made? Our purpose in the remainder of this chapter will be to answer the first, saving the second question for the next chapter.

## *The Meaning of Discipleship: What is a Disciple?*

The word translated as "make disciples" means "to bring [them] into the relation of pupil to teacher, 'taking his yoke' of authoritative instruction (Matt. 11:29), accepting what he says as true because he says it, and submitting to his requirements as right because he makes them."[20] In a simplified sense, it means to make someone into a learner or follower of Jesus Christ. Jesus' commission calls us to transform rebels into followers. Therefore, technically speaking, the Great Commission involves more than what is normally called evangelism.

### Decisions or Disciples?
The Great Commission produces disciples, not decisions. Becoming Christ's disciple does occur at a decisive point in time through a decision to receive Christ. But one of the sad evidences of a defective and unbiblical missions strategy is being satisfied with evangelistic decisions that yield no lasting fruit or transformation in the lives of those who have supposedly received Jesus Christ. While claiming to guard the gospel of grace, this approach actually denies the power of grace to convert the soul and to make the person who is in Christ

---

[20] Broadus, 593.

into a new creation (cf. 2 Cor. 5:17). Missions ought to produce more than decisions; it ought to produce disciples who follow Christ.

Jesus Himself taught in John 8:31-32: "If you continue in My word, then you are truly disciples of Mine; and you will know the truth, and the truth will make you free."

According to Jesus, a genuine disciple is one who continues in His word, and a disciple like that will "know the truth, and the truth will make you free." Christ speaks here of his freedom of salvation, not something beyond salvation. In verses 35-36 He describes this freedom as freedom from slavery to sin and the freedom of being God's children. Verse 51 makes the eternal significance of these words absolutely clear, "Truly, Truly, I say to you, if anyone keeps My word he will never see death."

Christ was speaking here to a group of people "who had believed Him" (v. 31), yet were, in Christ's own words, seeking to kill Him (v. 37). How could they be described as "believing" and still as slaves to sin and seeking to kill Jesus Christ? It was because their faith was not genuine; they were not true disciples of Jesus Christ. Carson summarizes the issue well:

> Jesus now lays down exactly what it is that separates spurious faith from true faith, fickle disciples from genuine disciples: *if you hold to my teaching, you are really my disciples.* The verb rendered "hold" is *meno*, to abide, to remain...In short, perseverance is the mark of true faith, of real disciples. A genuine believer remains in Jesus' "word" (*logos*), his teaching (*cf.* notes on 1:1): *i.e.* such a person obeys it, seeks to understand it better, and finds it more precious, more controlling, precisely when other forces flatly oppose it. It is the one who continues in the teaching who has both the Father and the Son (2 Jn. 9; *cf.* Heb. 3:14; Rev. 2:26).

In spite of efforts by some to deny the possibility of spurious faith, the Lord recognized that not all who claimed to follow Him were indeed true followers. His words here are no different than His warning in Matthew 7:21-23:

Not everyone who says to Me, "Lord, Lord," will enter the kingdom of heaven, but he who does the will of My Father who is in heaven will enter. Many will say to Me on that day, "Lord, Lord, did we not prophesy in Your name, and in Your name cast out demons, and in Your name perform many miracles?" And then I will declare to them, "I never knew you; depart from Me, you who practice lawlessness."

Please do not misunderstand the point here. In no way does Jesus teach that salvation is based on the performance or works of man. What is at stake in this debate is the power of the gospel—does it produce a new creation in Christ in the person who follows Him? We are not talking about the basis or condition of salvation. We are talking about the evidence of salvation. When God saves someone, He turns that person into a follower of Jesus Christ.

In calling believers to live out their faith in Jesus Christ, Paul reaffirms this perspective on the meaning of Christian discipleship. It is helpful to see him develop this argument in Ephesians 4:17-24:

So this I say, and affirm together with the Lord, that you walk no longer just as the Gentiles also walk, in the futility of their mind, being darkened in their understanding, excluded from the life of God because of the ignorance that is in them, because of the hardness of their heart; and they, having become callous, have given themselves over to sensuality for the practice of every kind of impurity with greediness. But you did not learn Christ in this way, if indeed you have heard Him and have been taught in Him, just as truth is in Jesus, that, in reference to your former manner of life, you lay aside the old self, which is being corrupted in accordance with the lusts of deceit, and that you be renewed in the spirit of your mind, and put on the new self, which in the likeness of God has been created in righteousness and holiness of the truth.

Although some have pointed to the fact that the word *disciple* is not used in the New Testament after the book of Acts to discredit the need for discipleship, this text raises serious question about the validity of this point. Verses 20-21, by their use of the words *learn,*

29

*heard*, and *been taught* are clearly teaching the concept of discipleship. In fact, the word translated "learn" is *manthano* and is used often in the gospels to express the nature of discipleship (e.g., Matt. 11:29, John 6:45 ff.). A standard Greek lexicon offers to "be someone's disciple" as an explanation of its meaning.[21]

Paul is arguing that the differences between the unbeliever and believer's manner of life (vv. 17-19) are grounded in who they are as Christ's disciples. To live like pagans is contradictory to having learned Christ, having heard Him, and having been taught in Him (vv. 20-21). Furthermore, when they did learn Christ, they were taught the radical difference between the former manner of life and the new self (vv. 22-24). The Ephesians "had been taught that becoming believers involves a radical break with the past, the putting off of the old person. The imagery of putting off the old person and putting on the new self is that of decisive change."[22] The combination of those last two words is crucial—biblical conversion is both decisive and transforming.

## Transaction or Transformation?

The core problem with much of evangelistic and missions emphasis is that it reduces conversion to a transaction—receiving Christ is like signing up for a life insurance policy—rather than presenting the full New Testament picture of spiritual transformation accomplished by God's power (e.g. 2 Cor. 5:17). This watered-down view of salvation has disastrous ramifications for the fulfillment of the Great Commission. It is out of harmony with the Scriptural presentation of what it means to receive Christ.

### We Preach Christ, Not Just What He Offers

The transactional approach to evangelism misses the point of the Lord's command to make disciples. The plain fact of Scripture is that the gospel is not primarily about salvation; it is about a Savior! The content of the gospel is more than an offer sheet or benefits package. It communicates who Jesus Christ is, what He did on the cross, what He offers to mankind by virtue of His victory over death,

---

[21] BAGD, p. 615.

[22] Andrew T. Lincoln, *Ephesians*, WBC (Dallas: Word, 1990), p. 284.

*and* what He demands of them (repentance and faith). Even the gospel summary in 1 Corinthians 15:3-4 focuses on Christ and His work, "For I delivered to you as of first importance what I also received, that Christ died for our sins according to the Scriptures, and that He was buried, and that He was raised on the third day according to the Scriptures." Christ is the focus of gospel preaching as presented in the New Testament. Consider these texts:

- And every day, in the temple and from house to house, they kept right on teaching and preaching Jesus as the Christ (Acts 5:42).
- But when Silas and Timothy came down from Macedonia, Paul began devoting himself completely to the word, solemnly testifying to the Jews that Jesus was the Christ (Acts 18:5).
- Now to Him who is able to establish you according to my gospel and the preaching of Jesus Christ, according to the revelation of the mystery which has been kept secret for long ages past (Rom. 16:25).
- But we preach Christ crucified, to Jews a stumbling block and to Gentiles foolishness (1 Cor. 1:23).
- For I determined to know nothing among you except Jesus Christ, and Him crucified (1 Cor. 2:2).
- In whose case the god of this world has blinded the minds of the unbelieving so that they might not see the light of the gospel of the glory of Christ, who is the image of God (2 Cor. 4:4).
- For we do not preach ourselves but Christ Jesus as Lord, and ourselves as your bond-servants for Jesus' sake (2 Cor. 4:5).

At the end of his earthly ministry, the Lord promised that He would send another Helper, the Spirit, and that "He will testify about" Christ (John 15:26). The Spirit magnifies Christ because Christ alone is the hope of salvation. Until a person sees the glory of Jesus Christ by faith in this life, he will never see the glory of Christ in heaven.

### *We Receive Christ, Not Just Facts about Christ*

This transactional approach to salvation also comes up short of what the Bible teaches about receiving the gospel of Jesus Christ. Many think that receiving the gospel is nothing more than an intellectual acceptance of certain biblical, historical facts. But that is not the biblical concept of accepting Jesus Christ as Lord and Savior. The Scriptures are clear that receiving Christ involves the mind, emotion, and will; in other words, it is a response of the complete person. We must know what the gospel is in order to be saved (mind), agree with it (emotion), and entrust ourselves to Jesus Christ in response to it (will).

Yes, we base our faith on biblical facts. Paul declares in Romans 10:14, "How then will they call on Him in whom they have not believed? How will they believe in Him whom they have not heard? And how will they hear without a preacher?" A morally responsible person cannot be saved apart from knowing about the person and work of Jesus Christ as revealed in Scripture: "faith comes from hearing, and hearing by the word of Christ" (Rom. 10:17).

But saving faith goes beyond mental comprehension of certain facts. Saving faith sees the glory of God in the face of Jesus Christ (2 Cor. 4:6). Saving faith involves a heart response to the gospel where the Spirit turns the affections to Christ in love. The apostle Peter provides clear insight into this aspect of saving faith:

> And though you have not seen Him, you love Him, and though you do not see Him now, but believe in Him, you greatly rejoice with joy inexpressible and full of glory, obtaining as the outcome of your faith the salvation of your souls (1 Pet. 1:8-9).

These verses formed the basis for Jonathan Edwards' classic, *Religious Affections*, in which he powerfully argued that "true religion, in great part, consists in holy affections."[23]

---

[23] *A Treatise Concerning Religious Affections* in *The Works of Jonathan Edwards*, 2 vols., rev. and ed. Edward Hickman (Carlisle, PA: Banner of Truth Trust, 1974), 1:236.

Saving faith also involves the will. That is, the believer embraces Jesus Christ as the only hope of eternal life and entrusts himself to Him. Paul confidently declared in 2 Timothy 1:12, "For this reason I also suffer these things, but I am not ashamed; for I know whom I have believed and I am convinced that He is able to guard what I have entrusted to Him until that day." Paul had entrusted himself to Christ, and he knew that Christ was completely trustworthy. This volitional aspect of saving faith is why the Scriptures speak of the "obedience of faith" (Rom. 1:5; 16:26) and of believing in Christ as obeying the Son (John 3:36) or heeding the good news (Rom. 10:16).

### *We Turn to Christ, We Do Not Simply Add Him to Life*

Sadly, many in our day are seeking to minimize or eliminate repentance from the gospel message. In removing or redefining repentance, they contradict what the Bible teaches about conversion. Conversion is the combination of turning from sin (repentance) and to Christ (faith) seen in texts like Acts 20:21, where Paul was "solemnly testifying to both Jews and Greeks of repentance toward God and faith in our Lord Jesus Christ." Although some have incorrectly used dispensationalism as a basis to argue that repentance was restricted to the Jews, this verse is clear that Paul preached it to Gentiles as well. In fact, in a strictly Gentile context, Mars Hill, Paul sets forth God's demand for repentance with unmistakable clarity, "Therefore having overlooked the times of ignorance, God is now declaring to men that all people everywhere should repent" (Acts 17:30). Note that it is "all people everywhere" who should repent. There can be no doubt or wavering on the fact that repentance is necessary for salvation.

Some, willing to concede that you must repent to be saved, have attempted to redefine repentance so that it is essentially no different from faith. They argue that the Greek word for repentance means nothing more than to change your mind—so repenting means you change your mind about Jesus Christ. You did not believe in Him, but now you do believe in Him. This argument fails on two counts. First, it is a flawed method of defining terms. While etymologies may be helpful in some cases, they are not necessarily the final word on the definition of a term; context and usage are. There is an old joke about Grape-Nuts that pointed out the fact that they are neither grapes nor nuts. Even if one argues that the word repentance comes from the two words "mind" and "change", it does not mean that all it means is change your mind in a purely intellectual sense.

More importantly, even if repentance meant nothing more than "change your mind," this view selectively chooses what you change your mind about. On what basis can they argue that it means only to change your mind about Christ? Why doesn't it include changing your mind about sin (cf. Luke 5:32; 15:7; Acts 2:38)? About God (cf. Acts 20:21)? About false worship (cf. Acts 17:30)? About dead works (cf. Heb. 6:1)? It is unacceptable to redefine the biblical concept of repentance in any way that excludes sin. At the heart of the gospel Jesus commissioned his disciples to preach is the message "that repentance for forgiveness of sins would be proclaimed in His name to all the nations, beginning from Jerusalem" (Luke 24:47).

If we eliminate repentance from the gospel, then we are not preaching the gospel of Jesus Christ. And if we have eliminated sin from our definition of repentance, then we are not preaching the kind of repentance that Jesus commissioned us to preach. The biblical gospel makes disciples who have turned to Christ, not simply added him to their collection of gods or squeezed Him into an unaltered life. This is why Paul could express confidence in the salvation of the Thessalonian believers:

> For they themselves report about us what kind of a reception we had with you, and how you turned to God from idols to serve a living and true God, and to wait for His Son from heaven, whom He raised from the dead, that is Jesus, who rescues us from the wrath to come (1 Thess. 1:9-10).

They demonstrated their faith through conversion. They turned from "idols" to "serve a living and true God." God will not accept a place on the shelf alongside of idols! As Jesus proclaimed, "No one can serve two masters; for either he will hate the one and love the other, or he will be devoted to one and despise the other. You cannot serve God and wealth" (Matt. 6:24). John's first letter states something similar:

> Do not love the world nor the things in the world. If anyone loves the world, the love of the Father is not in him. For all that is in the world, the lust of the flesh and the lust of the eyes and the boastful pride of life, is not from the Father, but is from the world. The world is passing away, and also its lusts; but the one who does the will of God lives forever (1 John 2:15-17).

While all believers will struggle with worldliness, a definitive break has occurred in the life of those who are saved. There are not two masters, only One.

Rather than simply changing our eternal destination (from hell to heaven), the Bible teaches that salvation is a work of spiritual transformation. As 2 Corinthians 5:17 makes plain, "if anyone is in Christ, he is a new creature; the old things passed away; behold, new things have come." Salvation involves the creation of a new nature that is evidenced in a changed life. As Paul writes in Ephesians 4:24, "and put on the new self, which in the likeness of God has been created in righteousness and holiness of the truth." God's saving power re-creates and transforms believers into His own likeness (cf. Col. 3:10).

The power of God's saving grace is so transforming that Paul can boldly warn those who are living in habitual sin of dire eternal consequences. Consider these often-neglected Scriptural warnings:

- Or do you not know that the unrighteous will not inherit the kingdom of God? Do not be deceived; neither fornicators, nor idolaters, nor adulterers, nor effeminate, nor homosexuals, nor thieves, nor the covetous, nor drunkards, nor revilers, nor swindlers, will inherit the kingdom of God (1 Cor. 6:9-10).
- Now the deeds of the flesh are evident, which are: immorality, impurity, sensuality, idolatry, sorcery, enmities, strife, jealousy, outbursts of anger, disputes, dissensions, factions, envying, drunkenness, carousing, and things like these, of which I forewarn you, just as I have forewarned you,

that those who practice such things will not inherit the kingdom of God (Gal. 5:19-21).

- For this you know with certainty, that no immoral or impure person or covetous man, who is an idolater, has an inheritance in the kingdom of Christ and God (Eph. 5:5).
- They profess to know God, but by their deeds they deny Him, being detestable and disobedient and worthless for any good deed (Titus 1:16).
- Pursue peace with all men, and the sanctification without which no one will see the Lord (Heb. 12:14).
- Little children, make sure no one deceives you; the one who practices righteousness is righteous, just as He is righteous; the one who practices sin is of the devil; for the devil has sinned from the beginning. The Son of God appeared for this purpose, to destroy the works of the devil. No one who is born of God practices sin, because His seed abides in him; and he cannot sin, because he is born of God (1 John 3:7-9).

Contrary to some popular teaching about salvation, the Bible is clear that we are saved not just from the penalty of sin, but also from its dominating power over our lives (Rom. 6:14). None of these texts are teaching that we keep ourselves saved by obedience, but they all teach that the evidence that we are indeed saved is that God has changed us. The new birth produces a new life, and where there is no new life, the biblical conclusion is that there has been no new birth.

### We Accept Christ, We Do Not Make a Deal for Eternal Life
The transactional evangelism approach also treats faith in Christ as a one-time belief in Christ, rather than a life of persevering attachment to Christ. While a person does express saving faith at a decisive point in time, it is wrong to conclude that saving faith does not necessarily last or continue. As surprising as it may seem, some even argue that a person could stop believing in Jesus Christ and still be saved. The Scriptures testify strongly against this unbiblical view of faith:

- Now I make known to you, brethren, the gospel which I preached to you, which also you received, in which also you stand, by which also you are saved, if you hold fast the word which I preached to you, unless you believed in vain (1 Cor. 15:1-2).

- And although you were formerly alienated and hostile in mind, engaged in evil deeds, yet He has now reconciled you in His fleshly body through death, in order to present you before Him holy and blameless and beyond reproach— if indeed you continue in the faith firmly established and steadfast, and not moved away from the hope of the gospel that you have heard, which was proclaimed in all creation under heaven, and of which I, Paul, was made a minister (Col. 1:21-23).
- But we are not of those who shrink back to destruction, but of those who have faith to the preserving of the soul (Heb. 10:39).

Please do not mistake the point here. I am not arguing that a person can lose his salvation. To the contrary, the Bible teaches that those who are saved "are protected by the power of God through faith for a salvation ready to be revealed in the last time" (1 Pet. 1:5). Precisely because it is God's power that protects them, we can say confidently with the apostle Paul "that He who began a good work in [them] will perfect it until the day of Christ Jesus" (Phil. 1:6). When God saves, His gracious power sustains the faith of His people until they reach their eternal home.

When looking from a human perspective, however, our only assurance that a person has truly trusted Christ is if they continue to hold fast to the gospel (1 Cor. 15:2) and to their confession of faith in Christ (Heb. 3:6, 14). In the words of the New Hampshire Confession of Faith, "That such only are real believers as endure unto the end; that their persevering attachment to Christ is the grand mark which distinguishes them from mere professors; that a special Providence watches over their welfare; and that they are kept by the power of God through faith unto salvation."[24]

---

[24] William L. Lumpkin, *Baptist Confessions of Faith*, rev. ed. (Valley Forge: Judson Press, 1969), 365.

That persevering attachment to Christ must characterize true conversion has significant implications for missions. Current approaches to missions too often concentrate only on the initial aspect of coming to Christ. Preoccupation with professions of faith seems to reveal that we are out of step with Paul in this matter, and, I would argue, it misses the point of the Great Commission—making disciples.

That Paul was vitally interested in more than mere professions of faith in Christ is clear from how he addresses the groups of believers among whom he had pioneered the gospel. In addition to the texts cited above in which he exhorted the believers in Corinth and Colossae to hold fast to the gospel, his concern over the spiritual welfare of the Thessalonians effectively demonstrates how he viewed the success of his missionary labors. He writes:

> Therefore when we could endure it no longer, we thought it best to be left behind at Athens alone, and we sent Timothy, our brother and God's fellow worker in the gospel of Christ, to strengthen and encourage you as to your faith, so that no one would be disturbed by these afflictions; for you yourselves know that we have been destined for this. For indeed when we were with you, we kept telling you in advance that we were going to suffer affliction; and so it came to pass, as you know. For this reason, when I could endure it no longer, I also sent to find out about your faith, for fear that the tempter might have tempted you, and our labor would be in vain (1 Thess. 3:1-5).

We know from the first chapter of this letter that the people of Thessalonica responded well to Paul's ministry, so we might be inclined to think, as we often do in our day, that it was a successful, complete missionary endeavor. But this text makes it clear that Paul was not prepared to come to that conclusion as quickly as we do. While he rejoiced at their initial reception of the gospel message, this passage makes it plain that the continued faith of the Thessalonians was essential for him to be sure his ministry had not been "in vain" (v. 5).

Paul knew and had forewarned them that following Christ would mean "afflictions." Because their afflictions came since they had converted to Christ, Paul was concerned that they might *be disturbed* by them (v. 3). The afflictions might shake their faith in Christ from its foundations. They might conclude, and others might try to convince them, that the trials were the result of foolishly following Paul's gospel. Paul's great concern in this whole section is seen in the repeated emphasis on faith (cf. 3:2, 5, 6, 7, 10). More specifically, he focuses on the solidity and continuation of their profession of faith. Phrases like "no one would be disturbed" (3:3), that his "labor would be in vain" (3:5), and that they "stand firm in the Lord" (3:8) reveal Paul's concern. Paul wanted them to continue in their Christian *faith*—eliminating the possibility that he thought human works or merit as the basis of their standing firm. Perseverance is not a matter of human works but of faith in God's promises. The real issue for Paul was whether they had come to Christ at all. If not, then his work in their midst was *vain* or empty. As Hiebert notes, "Paul was fully aware that the final outcome of his labors was dependent upon the steadfastness of his converts."[25]

A few years ago I heard a preacher illustrate the concept of receiving salvation by drawing a comparison between getting saved and getting on an airplane. Once you have boarded the plane, the preacher explained, you will arrive at the original destination whether you still want to or not. In the same way, he argued, once you have accepted the gift of eternal life, you will end up in heaven whether you still want to or not. I hope you are as shocked reading this as I was when I heard it. In a hopefully well-intentioned attempt to protect the doctrine of eternal security the preacher actually distorted the gospel and the biblical meaning of saving faith. This illustration perpetuates the false view that you only receive a ticket to heaven, not Christ Himself, when you profess faith in Christ. And instead of a faith that embraces Jesus Christ because it sees God's glory in His face (2 Cor. 4:6), this illustration presents us with a "faith" that does not continue until the day of Christ (Phil. 1:6) and therefore is not based in the power of God. This kind of one-time faith is not genuine saving faith.

---

[25] D. Edmond Hiebert, *The Thessalonian Epistles* (Chicago: Moody, 1971), 142.

The Apostle Paul would consider this illustration a tragic distortion of the gospel that undercuts the power of the gospel and the meaning of saving faith. It seems impossible to mesh its view of salvation with Paul's concern about the Thessalonians, Corinthians, and Colossians. If they had "boarded the plane" while he was preaching among them, then he would not have to be concerned whether his labor was in vain. But because he was after followers of Jesus Christ, in obedience to the Great Commission, he was very concerned that those who had professed faith in Christ demonstrate the genuineness of that profession by continuing to follow Christ. Or, as he makes clear in Colossians 1:28-29, he aimed for more than a profession of faith, he aimed at spiritual maturity: "We proclaim Him, admonishing every man and teaching every man with all wisdom, so that we may present every man complete in Christ. For this purpose also I labor, striving according to His power, which mightily works within me."

## *Summary and Implications*

The heart of the Great Commission is the command to make disciples, and loving obedience to Jesus Christ means that we must do what He has commanded. What He has commanded extends beyond simply preaching the gospel to lost people; it involves seeing rebels against God turned into followers of Jesus Christ. In contrast to the sometimes shallow approaches to evangelism and discipleship popular in our day, the New Testament presents us with a powerful gospel that focuses on Jesus Christ Himself, not just what He offers to sinners. And, rather than simply providing an eternal address change, the saving grace of God makes believers into new creatures, created to reflect God's image in righteousness and holiness. It is toward this purpose that we proclaim Christ.

The lack of true conversions and changed lives in our churches and on our mission fields is not a fault in the biblical gospel, but in the fact that we have watered it down by reducing saving faith to a business transaction and eliminated or redefined repentance. We have been preoccupied with short-term results (decisions) rather than life transformation (disciples). The net result of these shifts away from the biblical strategy is that much of professing Christianity, both in the United States and on the mission fields of the world, is a mile wide and an inch deep. Multitudes have prayed a prayer, but far fewer have received the Savior.

If we mean business about fulfilling the Great Commission then we need to stand without apology for a transforming gospel that calls people to repentance and faith. We must proclaim a gospel that calls people to turn from sin to a Savior, from dead works to Christ's righteousness, and from vain idols to the one true and living God as revealed in Jesus Christ. Christ commanded us to make disciples who would follow Him in baptism and obey all that He commanded. Our missions efforts must settle for nothing less.

*And when I came to you, brethren, I did not come with superiority of speech or of wisdom, proclaiming to you the testimony of God. For I determined to know nothing among you except Jesus Christ, and Him crucified.*

1 Corinthians 2:1-2

# 3

# THE TASK OF THE GREAT COMMISSION II: THE METHOD OF DISCIPLESHIP

Although Matthew 28:19-20 does not lay out a definitive process for making disciples, fulfilling its basic command requires us to understand how disciples are made. Historically the church has defined disciple-making process in the simple terms of evangelism or gospel proclamation. The church viewed the Great Commission as a mandate to proclaim the gospel to the ends of the earth. The other commission texts make the proclamation component explicit: "preach the gospel" (Mark 16:15), "that repentance for forgiveness of sins would be proclaimed in His name to all the nations" (Luke 24:47), "you shall be My witnesses" (Acts 1:8, cf. Luke 24:48), and "you will testify also" (John 15:27).

Proclaiming the good news of Jesus Christ was viewed as the key to making disciples, and, therefore, as the key to fulfilling the Great Commission. So it should not surprise us to find the book of Acts recording the disciple-making mission of the church in terms of the ministry of the Word. Perhaps the clearest text which joins these ideas is Acts 6:7, "The word of God kept on spreading; and the number of disciples continued to increase greatly in Jerusalem, and a great number of the priests were becoming obedient to the faith." This text makes clear the connection between the ministry of the Word (cf. 6:1-6) and the task of disciple making. Acts confirms this connection by repeatedly stressing the spread of the Word (e.g.,

12:24, 13:49, 19:20) and the priority of preaching (e.g., 6:4, 14:15, 15:35, 18:5, 28:31). Viewed from the perspective of Acts, the Great Commission's fulfillment was through the proclamation of the Word.

This emphasis is not restricted to the book of Acts. The Epistles reinforce this understanding of the Great Commission as well. In Romans 10:13-17, Paul unambiguously argues for the absolute necessity of verbal proclamation of the gospel if the work of missions is to be accomplished. The logic of his argument is airtight and irrefutable: since salvation is obtained only by explicit faith in Jesus Christ, then only those who have heard about and called upon Jesus Christ can be saved. This argument crescendos with the words, "so faith comes from hearing, and hearing by the word of Christ." And, based on vv. 14-15, both the word and the hearing are inseparably tied to a preacher.

In 1 Corinthians 1:17-2:5, Paul makes an extended argument for the importance of preaching the clear, undiluted gospel of the Cross. Apparently the sophisticated Corinthians desired something less offensive and "foolish" than this message and method. Yet, His defense of gospel proclamation proves that it is not simply one of the methods God intends to use to accomplish the Great Commission—it is the God-ordained method. The message of the Cross is the means by which the Great Commission is to be fulfilled.

The remarkable work of God in Thessalonica also confirms that the ministry of the Word is the key to fulfilling the Great Commission. Notice how Paul summarizes this work:

> For our gospel did not come to you in word only, but also in power and in the Holy Spirit and with full conviction; just as you know what manner of men we proved to be among you for your sake. You also became imitators of us and of the Lord, having received the word in much tribulation with the joy of the Holy Spirit, so that you became an example to all the believers in Macedonia and in Achaia. For the word of the Lord sounded forth from you, not only in Macedonia and Achaia, but also in every place your faith toward God

has gone forth, so that we have no need to say anything (1 Thess. 1:5-8).

The Word is central to all that happens in this passage. Paul describes his apostolic ministry in terms of the Word and the conversion of the Thessalonians as their receiving the Word. The powerful transformation that the Word produced in them made them into a model group of believers because the Word sounded out from them. They became Christians through the Word and they lived like Christians by giving out the Word. No wonder Paul requested these same believers to "pray for us that the word of the Lord will spread rapidly and be glorified, just as it did also with you" (2 Thess. 3:1).

## The Shifting Shape of Evangelical Missions

The evidence that gospel proclamation and the ministry of the Word is the fulfillment of the Great Commission is overwhelming, yet there has been a considerable shift in missions thinking and literature away from this position. This shift is out of step with the Scriptures and seriously threatens the fulfillment of Christ's commission to His church. We cannot deny or ignore this threat any longer.

### Mission or Missions?

When considering the decline of missions movements like the Student Volunteer Movement in the 19th century, one major error is the shift from proclamation evangelism to so-called larger or holistic evangelism.[26] Sadly, evangelicalism has retraced these downward steps in the years since the Congress for World Evangelization was held in Lausanne, Switzerland in 1974. Prior to the conference, there was considerable debate about the relationship between evangelism and social action. Some considered that debate to be the "unfinished business" of the last major evangelical conference on evangelism which met in Berlin during 1966.[27] In the

---

[26] See chapter two of this book. Cf. also Arthur Johnston, *The Battle of World Evangelism* (Wheaton, IL: Victor, 1978).

[27] Johnston, 221.

eight years between these conferences, evangelicals moved significantly in the direction of social action. Consider the positive assessment of Edward Dayton:

> In the eight years between Berlin and Lausanne, there was tremendous movement in the evangelical part of Christ's church…. Lausanne was intended to be a congress of those involved in trying to reach the world; but the Holy Spirit was also enlivening the minds of men and women to expand our understanding of what it meant to evangelize. The Lausanne Covenant greatly broadened our worldviews. We were called to see that the task of evangelization was not confined to the sharing of information about Jesus. There was a life to be lived. We saw the need for the broad redemption of the world in all its aspects…. The year of Lausanne—1974— might also be described as a watershed year in Western evangelicals' interest in social concerns.[28]

What Dayton considers to be progress, I contend was regress—a return to the flawed thinking of the ecumenical movement that had embraced a social agenda over evangelism.

Perhaps the chief architect and proponent of this shift in thinking was John Stott, a prolific writer and leader for the Lausanne Movement. From his work on the publication of the Lausanne Covenant and its attending exposition and commentary to his own books on this issue, Stott set the agenda for inclusion of a social action agenda among evangelicals. He set out to do this to counter the past failure of evangelicalism. In his words:

> One of the most notable features of the worldwide evangelical movement during the last ten to fifteen years (c. 1970-1985) has been the recovery of our temporarily mislaid social conscience. For approximately fifty years (c. 1920-70) evangelical Christians were preoccupied with the task of

---

[28] Edward R. Dayton, "Social Transformation: The Mission of God" in *The Church in Response to Human Need*, ed. Vinay Samuel and Christopher Sugden (Grand Rapids: Eerdmans, 1987), 53.

defending the historic biblical faith against the attacks of theological liberalism, and reacting against its "social gospel." But now we are convinced that God has given us social as well as evangelistic responsibilities in his world.[29]

Stott, confirming Dayton's assessment, pinpoints Lausanne as the "turning-point for the worldwide evangelical constituency" because it set forth the principle that both evangelism and socio-political involvement are part of the Christian duty.[30]

How did the "worldwide evangelical constituency" come to see that socio-political involvement was part of the Christian duty? The pivotal shift in thinking was demonstrated and advanced by the redefinition of the Christian mission. Historically, the terms *mission* and *missionary* focused our attention on the evangelistic/discipleship mandate given to us by the Lord. Stott, and others, called for a redefinition of that term so that mission summarized all "that Christ sends His people into the world to do" and that this "cannot be limited to proclamation evangelism."[31] More directly, he argues:

> Instead of seeking to evade our social responsibility, we need to open our ears and listen to the voice of him who calls his people in every age to go out into the lost and lonely world (as he did), in order to live and love, to witness and serve, like him and for him. For that is "mission." Mission is our human response to the divine commission. It is the whole Christian lifestyle, including both evangelism and social responsibility, dominated by the conviction that Christ sends us out into the world as the Father sent him into the world, and that into the world we must therefore go—to live and work for him.[32]

---

[29] John Stott, *Decisive Issues Facing Christians Today*, 2nd ed. (Grand Rapids: Revell, 1990), xi.

[30] Ibid., 9-10.

[31] John Stott, *The Contemporary Christian* (Downers Grove, IL: InterVarsity, 1992), 342.

[32] Stott, *Decisive Issues*, 15.

For Stott, the Christian mission is dual: evangelism and social action. This subtle shift in terminology, missions to mission, represented an enormous shift in theology and philosophy.

Though Lausanne articulated a logical priority for evangelism, it clearly argued that *both* evangelism and social action are parts of the Christian mission. The Lausanne Covenant went so far as to "express penitence both for our neglect and for having sometimes regarded evangelism and social concern as mutually exclusive."[33] The exposition and commentary on these words go even further:

> *We express penitence both for our neglect of* our Christian social responsibility and for our naïve polarization in *having sometimes regarded evangelism and social concern as mutually exclusive.* This confession is mildly worded. A large group at Lausanne, concerned to develop a radical Christian discipleship, expressed themselves more strongly, "We must repudiate as demonic the attempt to drive a wedge between evangelism and social action."[34]

So what actually surfaces is less two distinct parts of one mission, and more two activities that cannot be separated from each other; that is, as we do one, we do the other. Further work by the Lausanne Movement fleshed out the details of the relationship between evangelism and social action. In 1982, *The Grand Rapids Report on Evangelism and Social Responsibility* elaborated a threefold relationship:

> First, social activity is a *consequence* of evangelism. That is, evangelism is the means by which God brings people to new birth, and their new life manifests itself in service to others.... We can go further than this, however. Social responsibility is more than the consequence of evangelism; it is also one of its principal aims.

---

[33] John Stott, ed., *Making Christ Known: Historic Mission Documents from the Lausanne Movement 1974-1989* (Grand Rapids: Eerdmans, 1996), 24.
[34] Ibid., 24.

Secondly, social activity can be a *bridge* to evangelism. It can break down prejudice and suspicion, open closed doors, and gain a hearing for the Gospel. Jesus himself sometimes performed works of mercy before proclaiming the good news of the kingdom...

Thirdly, social activity not follows evangelism as its consequence and aim, and precedes it as its bridge, but also accompanies it as its *partner*. They are like the two blades of a pair of scissors or the two wings of a bird. This partnership is clearly seen in the public ministry of Jesus, who not only preached the Gospel but fed the hungry and healed the sick. In his ministry, *kerygma* (proclamation) and *diakonia* (service) went hand in hand. His words explained his works, and his works dramatized his words. Both were expressions of his compassion for people, and both should be ours....

Thus, evangelism and social responsibility, while distinct from one another, are integrally related in our proclamation of and obedience to the Gospel. The partnership is, in reality, a marriage.[35]

Given this frame of reference, it is not surprising, then, to find one of the members of this consultation draw the following conclusion: "And what is social transformation for the Christian? Is it not the entire business that God is about, namely, the redemption of the world? And is not the mission of the church social transformation in every dimension?"[36]

### *Incarnation or Proclamation?*

As you may have noticed in the previous section, much (if not all) of the basis for the transition from missions to mission is said to be based on the example of Jesus Christ. John Stott especially has set forth the argument that two texts from John's Gospel form the proper basis for the Christian mission: "As You sent Me into the

---

[35] Ibid., 181-182.

[36] Dayton, "Social Transformation: The Mission of God," 54.

world, I also have sent them into the world" and "Peace be with you; as the Father has sent Me into the world, I also send you" (John 17:18 and 20:21 respectively). Commenting on the Lausanne Covenant, Stott writes:

> The opening affirmation echoes the prayer and the commission of Jesus (John 17:18; 20:21): *we affirm that Christ sends his redeemed people into the world as the Father sent him.* It recognizes that Christ's mission in the world is to be the model of the church's (NB, the "as-so" in both texts), and that *this calls for a similar deep and costly penetration of the world.*[37]

The backbone of Stott's position is the "as-so" language in these two texts. He understands this language to establish a model for our mission, an incarnational model.

> For if the Christian mission is to be modeled on Christ's mission, it will surely involve for us, as it did for him, an entering into other people's worlds.... Incarnational mission, whether evangelistic or social or both, necessitates a costly identification with people in their actual situations.[38]

In another place he develops the argument further:

> Nor do I feel able to withdraw the conviction that our mission is to be modeled on Christ's. Just as his love for us is like the Father's love for him, so his sending us into the world is like his Father's sending him into the world. If words and works went together in his ministry, they should also in ours.[39]

Stott does not hesitate to establish these texts as teaching *the* normative pattern for mission:

---

[37] John Stott, *Making Christ Known*, 29.

[38] *Decisive Issues*, 21-22.

[39] *The Contemporary Christian*, 342.

Now he sends us into the world, as the Father sent him into the world. In other words, our mission is to be modeled on his. Indeed, all authentic mission is incarnational mission. It demands identification without loss of identity. It means entering other people's worlds, as he entered ours, though without compromising our Christian convictions, values or standards.... That is the principle of incarnation. It is identification with people where they are.[40]

These two modifications in definitions dramatically altered the landscape of evangelical missions. The shift from missions to mission opened the door to an aggressive social action agenda, legitimized as an essential part of the Christian mission. The reshaping of the Christian mission into an incarnational, rather than proclamational model solidified the view that our words and works have equal place in witness. In fact, without the works, according to this view, our words will lack credibility.

I have taken pains, and considerable space, to present this position carefully for two reasons. First, as a matter of procedure, we must know what is being said before we can evaluate it properly. I have no interest in destroying a straw man, so I wanted to allow you to see what has been said so you can evaluate both it and my critique of it. Second, and perhaps of greater concern to me, is the fact that I have heard many of these same arguments beginning to filter their way into fundamentalist preaching and teaching on missions and evangelism. In showing where this language and these concepts originated and where they have led, my hope is that it will cause us to think very carefully about the far-reaching ramifications of simple-sounding shifts in terms and concepts.

## *Evaluating Holistic Mission and the Incarnational Model*

So what is wrong with Stott's definition of mission and articulation of the incarnational model for ministry? I believe we should begin

---

[40] Ibid., 358.

by questioning the somewhat arbitrary choice to make John 17:18 and 20:21 the definitive texts regarding mission. In light of the unmistakable emphasis in all of the other commission texts on proclamation, it seems very strained to redefine mission on the basis of these two somewhat obscure texts. By obscure, I mean that they do not specify the nature of our commission, that is, they do not at all tell us *what* we are to do. In terms of biblical interpretation, the proper way to approach the issue of mission would be to correlate all of the commission texts by moving from the clearest texts to the more obscure. For some reason, Stott actually works in the other direction. Matthew 28:19-20, Mark 16:15, Luke 24:47, and Acts 1:8 are all to be made to fit inside of the incarnational model. But the focus in each of the other texts is clearly on proclamation, not incarnation. The proper method of study would be to determine how John 17:18 and 20:21 fit into what the other texts say.

But even if we accept Stott's argument that these two verses establish the biblical paradigm for missions, his claim that these texts are intended to teach an incarnational model for missions is mistaken. By choosing to focus on the two words "as-so" Stott misses the point of these texts. Viewed in the larger context of John's gospel, the focus is clearly on the words "sent" (17:18) and "sent/send" (20:21). In fact, by focusing on the "as-so" portion Stott turns the entire discussion into how Jesus came, not how He was sent by the Father, yet the "sending" is the point of the texts. Just as Jesus was sent by His Father to do the Father's will, the disciples are now commissioned by the Son to do His will and carry out His work. John 4:34 provides the backdrop for this language and concept, "Jesus said to them, 'My food is to do the will of Him who sent Me and to accomplish His work.'" The language of sending (used 41 times in John's Gospel) communicates delegated authority and responsibility for obedience on the part of the one sent.[41] In Jesus' case, He demonstrated His complete dependence upon and total obedience to the Father.[42] If there is a model presented for the

---

[41] Andreas J. Kostenberger, *The Mission of Jesus and the Disciples According to the Fourth Gospel* (Grand Rapids: Eerdmans, 1998), 107.

[42] Donald A. Carson, *The Gospel According to John* (Grand Rapids: Eerdmans, 1991), 648.

disciples here, this is it—we are to walk in dependence upon and obedience to Jesus Christ, since He is now the Sender and we are the sent ones.

Of particular interest is the connection in John's Gospel between the language of sending/going and the themes of harvest, fruit-bearing, and witness.[43] For example:

- I sent you to reap that for which you have not labored; others have labored and you have entered into their labor (4:38).
- You did not choose Me but I chose you, and appointed you that you would go and bear fruit, and that your fruit would remain, so that whatever you ask of the Father in My name He may give to you (15:16).
- When the Helper comes, whom I will send to you from the Father, that is the Spirit of truth who proceeds from the Father, He will testify about Me, and you will testify also, because you have been with Me from the beginning (15:26-27).

The key to understanding what Jesus meant in 17:18 and 20:21 is the use of the "sent" idea in 4:34-38. There Jesus, in an evangelistic context, says that "His food is to do the will of Him who sent Me and to accomplish His work." Growing out of His own commitment to do His Father's will (that is, participate in the harvest, cf. vv. 35-37), He sends the disciples into the harvest (v. 38).

Even the immediate context of John 17:18 and 20:21 makes it clear that Jesus is not commissioning His disciples to engage in social action. That idea is completely foreign to the context of these texts, and to import it from other passages in the Gospels is not legitimate. As Carson notes, "To appeal to several verses from Luke to establish what is central to John's understanding of mission is indefensible."[44] We should be asking, what do the immediate contexts of these verses tell us about the mission Jesus has in mind for the disciples? If we look in John 17 for the answer to that question, we don't have to

---

[43] Kostenberger, 141.

[44] Carson, 648.

look too far to see that the mission of Jesus was to make the Father's name known to the disciples by giving them His word. Verses 4-6 make this clear:

> I glorified You on the earth, having accomplished the work which You have given Me to do. Now, Father, glorify Me together with Yourself, with the glory which I had with You before the world was. I have manifested Your name to the men whom You gave Me out of the world; they were Yours and You gave them to Me, and they have kept Your word.

It is crucial to see the connections here: 1) Jesus did the "work" He was sent to do; 2) that work is described as manifesting the Father's name to the men given to Christ "out of the world" (v. 6); and 3) the fact that they were given to Christ is evidenced by their having "kept" the Father's word. So, in context, the sending that Jesus has in mind, if it is patterned after His, is a sending that involves the manifestation of Christ's name through the Word. This is confirmed by the emphasis on the word in verses 8, 14, 17, and especially 20, where Jesus says, "I do not ask on behalf of these alone, but for those also who believe in Me *through their word.*" The focus of this passage is not on the incarnation; it is on the proclamation of God's Word.

The same may be said about the context of 20:21. While it is a very complicated passage, the text following the sending language immediately addresses the issue of forgiveness of sins, not works of mercy or service. The symbolic bestowal of the Spirit (v. 22) is tied to the commission in v. 21.[45] The Spirit's ministry is presented throughout John's Gospel as clearly connected to the task of witnessing (cf. 3:34; 15:26-27; 16:7-11), not to mention that both Luke and Acts tie the reception of the Spirit to the task of witnessing (Luke 24:47-49; Acts 1:8).

There is simply nothing in the contexts of these verses to make an argument for social action. To the contrary, the context clearly establishes that the disciples were being sent by Jesus Christ to bear witness to Him and that others would believe on Jesus through their

---

[45] As the words, "And when He had said this" indicate, cf. Carson, 649.

word. Kostenberger states the case against Stott's position quite forthrightly:

> The notion of the disciples' mission as "service to humanity" founded on the model of Jesus' mission appears, contrary to Stott's assertions, to be inconsistent with the Fourth Gospel's teaching on mission. A focus on human service and on human need, though often characteristic of contemporary mission practice, is not presented in the Fourth Gospel as the primary purpose of either Jesus' or the disciples' mission.[46]

Alongside of these textually governed arguments for rejecting Stott's view, we must add two theological arguments. First, the connection that Stott draws between the works of Jesus Christ and social action is very weak. The Lord's works were miracles—He fed the hungry by turning a few loaves of bread and fish into enough to feed thousands as a display of supernatural power. The leap from that to opening a soup kitchen is woefully simplistic and stretches credibility. To move from miraculous healings to providing medical services is, from my perspective, equally suspect. His miracles were unique and served the special purpose of authenticating His Messiahship (cf. Matt. 11:4-5; John 2:11). There can be no doubt that Jesus was moved with compassion by the hurts and needs of people, but it is wrong to conclude that the miracles were primarily a matter of compassion. The Lord of Glory clearly possessed sufficient power to heal everyone, but did not.

Against the kind of argument that Stott and others make are the very words of Jesus Himself when confronted with the pressing needs of people. Mark 1:36-38 establishes the proper place of Christ's miracles in His overall ministry:

> Simon and his companions searched for Him; they found Him, and said to Him, "Everyone is looking for You." He said to them, "Let us go somewhere else to the towns nearby, so that I may preach there also; for that is what I came for."

---

[46] *The Mission of Jesus and the Disciples*, 215.

Here the self-confessed purpose of Jesus is to preach; in His words, "that is what I came for." Those words fit perfectly with what we saw in John 4:34-38 and especially John 17:4-6. The words and works of Jesus were not on equal footing; the works served the words.

A second theological concern is Stott's use of the language of incarnation to describe our mission and ministry. To state the concern bluntly, the incarnation is an unrepeatable and unique miracle that should not be trivialized by calling it a "cross cultural journey" or comparing it to the "Apollo mission to the moon."[47] Scripturally, the Son of God became incarnate (was made "flesh and blood") so that He could "make propitiation for the sins of the people" (cf. Heb. 2:14-17). He had to become incarnate because He existed immaterially from all eternity; by definition, human beings are already incarnate! Stott's language sounds nice, but in reality, the "incarnation" of which he speaks is reduced to identifying with those to whom you minister. This reduction seems to cheapen the incredible miracle of the incarnation that is presented to us in Scripture. Kostenberger, again, provides a profound critique of Stott:

> Stott, by focusing on Jesus' *incarnation* as a model for the church's mission, seems to be at odds with the Fourth Gospel's presentation of Jesus' incarnation as thoroughly unique, unprecedented, and unrepeatable (cf. especially the designation *monogenes* in 1:14, 18; 3:14, 18). The incarnation is linked with Jesus' eternal preexistence (cf. 1:1, 14) and his unique relationship with the Father (cf. 1:14, 18).[48]

The bottom line is that the incarnation distinctly and uniquely pertains to Jesus Christ. And as others have properly noted, if Stott can call for the church to adopt an incarnational model based on John 17:18 and 20:21, why does he not call us to imitate Christ's atonement? On what basis does he choose between the two?[49] I believe his choices are controlled by his agenda, not the text. In his

---

[47] Stott, *The Contemporary Christian*, 357.

[48] *The Mission of Jesus and the Disciples*, 216.

[49] Kostenberger, 216; Johnston, 406.

zeal to promote social action, he has forced a lot of excess baggage into two Bible verses and a theological concept. It is time for us to drop the baggage and return to the clear command of Jesus Christ to be His witnesses.

## *A Renewed Commitment to the Great Commission*

What I have been writing flows out of one very important, deep conviction: the mission that Jesus Christ has given to His church cannot be fulfilled apart from the proclamation of the Word. It is also based in a very deep concern: the contemporary church is losing sight of this truth and many are losing the resolve to stand against this terrible tide. What we have studied in this chapter has some very important implications for the task of missions.

First, we cannot fall prey to the idea that the Great Commission means evangelism alone, especially if it is cut off from discipleship. Christ has commanded us to make disciples, not count up evangelistic decisions. If all we have is a choice between getting the gospel to a group of people in a one-time shot or doing nothing, obviously, we should take the one-time shot and trust God to do the rest. But it is not legitimate to turn that decision into a ministry goal or guideline. The Great Commission is not fulfilled until there are disciples who continue to obey the teachings of Jesus Christ and bear fruit through Him. We must consistently make that our objective, strategizing and striving toward that end.

Second, the main, if not exclusive, thrust of any missions program must be the establishment of long-term discipleship that results in an indigenous and self-perpetuating church movement. We will say more about this in the next chapter, but let it be said plainly here that the proper focus of all missionary activity must be on the spread of the Word, for it, through the work of the Spirit, is the power that produces disciples.

These concepts have important implications for missionaries. Preaching the Word must be in the forefront of all missionary endeavors. And training pastors/preachers is essential work for missionaries since the spread of the gospel in any region is dependent, from a human perspective, on their ministry. Finally, all missionaries should be evangelists in the truest sense of the term, preachers of the gospel of Jesus Christ calling men and women to repentance and faith in Him.

*I write so that you will know how one ought to conduct himself in the household of God, which is the church of the living God, the pillar and support of the truth.*

1 Timothy 3:15

# 4

# THE TARGET OF THE GREAT COMMISSION

There is an old traveler's joke about an airline pilot who informs the passengers over the plane's public-address system that he has both good and bad news. The good news is that they are making excellent time, and the bad news is that they are lost! To be blunt, it seems that the contemporary church's approach to missions is like that pilot's news—we are making great time, but not always sure where we are headed. Melvin Hodges expresses my concern well:

> It would be logical to suppose that all the different aspects of the outreach of the church in foreign lands would be united by a common goal. Yet, what a variety of answers would be evoked were we to ask missionaries of the Christian faith throughout the world to define their goal![50]

The purpose of this chapter is to focus on the target, or goal, of the Great Commission. Without a clear understanding of the God-assigned target, we will be tempted to substitute activity for accomplishment, to be satisfied that we are busy doing missions without really being sure that we are doing exactly what Jesus commissioned us to do. I believe Hodges is correct again to assert, "Our ultimate goal and the means which we employ to reach the goal are intricately related. If our goal is not clearly defined we may

---

[50] Melvin L. Hodges, *The Indigenous Church* (Springfield, MO: Gospel Publishing House, 1976), 9.

err in the choice of methods employed and fail to realize the true fruit of our labors."[51]

This chapter argues from the Scriptures that the true target of the Great Commission is establishing local churches, not merely winning people to Jesus Christ. The *task* of the Great Commission, as we saw in the last two chapters, is making and maturing disciples. But the task is a means toward the goal of building local assemblies of disciples who will carry out the Great Commission themselves. The Great Commission starts with winning people to Christ, it continues in discipleship, and culminates in thriving local churches. The true measure of success is churches planted, not converts won.

Although at first sight such a distinction may seem to be splitting hairs, I believe the ramifications of it for missions and missionaries are significant. Your goal determines your strategy. If the goal is to win as many people to Christ as possible, then that will translate into different strategies than if the goal is to see local churches planted. Someone might argue that establishing local churches should translate into winning more people to Christ; so winning converts is actually the target. However, I would argue that this outcome is actually the result of the missionary's having reached the target point—a growing, reproducing church has been planted. At that point, the indigenous church is no longer the object of Great Commission ministry; it becomes a participant in it!

## The Proof of the Great Commission Target of Church Planting

How can we be sure that church planting is the ultimate target of the Great Commission? This section will reexamine the commission text and then consider the larger context of the New Testament Scriptures to argue five powerful reasons that the target of the Great Commission is the establishment of growing, reproducing local churches.

---

[51] Ibid., 9-10.

- The Content of the Great Commission: Church planting is the necessary context for the two central components of disciple-making—baptizing and teaching.
- The Backdrop of the Great Commission: Church planting is the work Christ declares he is accomplishing through his people's obedience.
- The Implementation of the Great Commission: Church planting is the main activity of the book of Acts.
- The Description of the Great Commission: Church planting and strengthening is the focus of Paul's missionary efforts, letters, and prayers.
- The Fulfillment of the Great Commission: Church planting was considered the mark of a reached area.

## *The Content of the Great Commission*

Church planting is the necessary context for the two central components of disciple-making—baptizing and teaching. These components communicate a responsibility that clearly goes beyond bringing a person to faith in Christ: publicly identifying with Christ and learning the teachings of Christ. As we noted in examining the task of missions, a person who has not been baptized and who does not hold fast to the apostolic teaching may not be a genuine believer.

So how do I come to the conclusion that these activities must happen in the context of the local church? Consider Acts 2:41-42:

> So then, those who had received his word were baptized; and that day there were added about three thousand souls. They were continually devoting themselves to the apostles' teaching and to fellowship, to the breaking of bread and to prayer.

The threefold pattern of Matthew 28 is here in this text: evangelism ("received his word"), incorporation into the body of believers ("were baptized...there were added"), and instruction ("apostles' teaching"). The commission clearly entails more than evangelism, if evangelism is strictly defined as leading someone to a profession of faith in Jesus Christ, and the opening pages of church history confirm this. Those who professed faith in Christ identified with Him in baptism and brought themselves under His teaching through the Apostles.

In fact, the apostle Paul, writing to the believers at Ephesus, makes clear that the Lord's plan for the time until He returns involves the "official" function of pastor-teachers "for the equipping of the saints for the work of service, to the building up of the body of Christ" (Eph. 4:12). The Lord Jesus has provided gifted men to lead the church in fulfilling the Great Commission responsibility of "teaching them to observe all that I commanded you."

The local church is the God-ordained means for the baptizing and instructing of those who have professed faith in Jesus Christ. Without the formation of local assemblies, the commission cannot be fulfilled. When we accept Christ, we are brought into union with Him and placed into His body, the church. Though the "church" is the mystical, universal Body of Christ, the responsibilities of baptizing and teaching belong to the local church as visible expression of that Body. Thus church planting must be the target of missions.

## The Backdrop of the Great Commission

Church planting is the work Christ declares he is accomplishing through his people's obedience. Before we leave the Gospels to consider how Acts and the Epistles detail the local church orientation of the Great Commission, it is beneficial to consider the backdrop found in Christ's words in Matthew 16:18. In response to Peter's confession that He is "the Christ, the Son of the living God," the Lord Jesus proclaims, "I also say to you that you are Peter, and upon this rock I will build My church; and the gates of Hades will not overpower it."

While there is considerable debate about the identity of "the rock" upon which Christ will build the church, that Christ prophesied the church's establishment is clear. The prophetic nature of this word is evident from the words "I *will* build." Christ, at the time when this was spoken, was not yet building His church. In light of the prophetic nature of this text, its correlation to Matthew 28:19-20 seems clear. The Great Commission is the means by which Christ will build His church. He, on the basis of His post-resurrection authority, commissions them to engage in the work of making disciples and forming them into assemblies where they can be instructed to follow the Lord.

Missions is Christ's work through His people to reach His sheep—a work He announced during His earthly ministry and joined to the witness of His disciples. In John 10:16, the Lord declared, "I have other sheep, which are not of this fold: I must bring them also, and they will hear My voice; and they will become one flock with one shepherd." This is clearly a prophecy about the Gentile mission. Jesus anticipated the work of missions prior to His death and resurrection and spoke of His purpose to call out sheep ("they will hear My voice") from the nations of the earth. In His high priestly prayer, the Lord indicates how He will call out these sheep as He prays not only for the disciples, but also for "those also who will believe in Me through their word" (John 17:20).

Although we must obey the commission, it is still Christ who builds the church! In Romans Paul, speaking about his missionary endeavors, demonstrates that it is Christ at work through the missionary, "For I will not presume to speak of anything except what Christ has accomplished through me, resulting in the obedience of the Gentiles by word and deed" (Rom. 15:18).

The combination of these texts shows that Jesus anticipated the work of missions that would be given to the disciples in what we call the Great Commission. Matthew 16:18 ties that work to the building of the church. Thus Church planting is the target of missions.

### The Implementation of the Great Commission

Church planting is also the main activity of the book of Acts, the historical record of the first activities fulfilling the Great Commission. We have already noted the pattern in Acts 2: evangelism, incorporation into the assembly of believers, and devotion to the apostolic teaching. After Pentecost, the church at

Jerusalem was established as a growing "congregation of those who believed" (4:32).

When the gospel spread to Antioch, the task of making "disciples of all the nations" began. Acts 11:20-21 says, "But there were some of them, men of Cyprus and Cyrene, who came to Antioch and began speaking to the Greeks also, preaching the Lord Jesus. And the hand of the Lord was with them, and a large number who believed turned to the Lord." In the words of Matthew 28:19, they were making disciples of the Lord Jesus Christ ("turned to the Lord"), and, in fulfillment of Matthew 28:20, the Lord was with them in the task ("the hand of the Lord was with them").

When word of this dramatic growth spread to the church in Jerusalem, Barnabas was sent to check things out (Acts 11:22). Barnabas rejoiced at the grace of God displayed in the saving of these Gentiles, and he moved quickly to strengthen the work by enlisting Saul's assistance. Barnabas and Saul stayed with the church in Antioch an entire year and "taught considerable numbers; and the disciples were first called Christians in Antioch." Great Commission work in Antioch resulted in a church that could carry out the commission themselves, "teaching them to observe all that [Christ] commanded."

The work in Antioch was a normative pattern for the Apostles' activity as Acts 14:21-23 demonstrates:

> After they had preached the gospel to that city and had made many disciples, they returned to Lystra and to Iconium and to Antioch, strengthening the souls of the disciples, encouraging them to continue in the faith, and saying, "Through many tribulations we must enter the kingdom of God." When they had appointed elders for them in every church, having prayed with fasting, they commended them to the Lord in whom they had believed.

The apostolic missionary practice was evangelism ("preached the gospel...made many disciples"), the edification of the saints ("strengthening the souls of the disciples"), and the establishment of local churches ("appointed elders for them in every church"). Any view of missions that reduces it to merely evangelizing lost people simply fails to account adequately for the missionary practice of the early church. The work of disciple-making demanded the establishment of local assemblies that provide opportunity for worship, fellowship, edification, and the continuation of evangelistic outreach.

## The Description of the Great Commission

Church planting and strengthening was the focus of Paul's missionary efforts, letters, and prayers (cf. Acts 11:19-26 and 14:21-23). His church planting efforts at Corinth serve as a good window into how Paul viewed his Great Commission activity. Acts 18 provides the historical record of the Corinthian church's founding, and in 1 Corinthians 3:4-17, Paul offers an inspired commentary on the church planting process:

> For when one says, "I am of Paul," and another, "I am of Apollos," are you not mere men? What then is Apollos? And what is Paul? Servants through who you believed, even as the Lord gave opportunity to each one. I planted, Apollos watered, but God was causing the growth. So then neither the one who plants nor the one who waters is anything, but God who causes the growth. Now he who plants and he who waters are one; but each will receive his own reward according to his own labor. For we are God's fellow workers; you are God's field, God's building. According to the grace which was given to me, like a wise master builder I laid a foundation, and another is building on it. But each man must be careful how he builds on it. For no man can lay a foundation other than the one which is laid, which is Jesus Christ. Now if any man builds on the foundation with gold, silver, precious stones, wood, hay, straw, each man's work will become evident; for the day will show it because it is to be revealed with fire, and the fire itself will test the quality of each man's work. If any man's work which he has built on it remains, he will receive a reward. If any man's work is burned up, he will suffer loss; but he himself will be saved,

yet so as through fire. Do you not know that you are a temple of God and that the Spirit of God dwells in you? If any man destroys the temple of God, God will destroy him, for the temple of God is holy, and that is what you are.

As Paul confronts the church's carnality and party spirit, he recounts how the church was established in Corinth. The Corinthians were dividing into camps claiming, "I am of Paul" and "I am of Apollos" (v. 4). Against this divisive rhetoric, Paul argues that both Apollos and Paul are only "servants through whom you believed" (v. 5) and that, "I planted, Apollos watered, but God was causing the growth" (v. 6). His basic point is that the human instruments that God uses should not be the focus, God Himself should be.

Paul's description is important to our study. Although it is common to take the words, "I planted, Apollos watered, but God was causing the growth," as referring to the process of evangelism, the context and historical record of Acts make it clear that these words speak of church planting. Paul served as the church planter, and Apollos followed his ministry in Corinth and nurtured the work that the Apostle Paul began (cf. Acts 19:1). Both men served God faithfully, but God is the One who caused the church at Corinth to grow. It is true that evangelism is a process that involves sowing and reaping (cf. John 4:34-38), but 1 Corinthians 3:6 is referring to church planting, not the evangelistic process.

Further confirmation of this focus is found in v. 10. Having referred, in v. 9, to the Corinthians as "God's field, God's building," Paul describes his own ministry in construction terms. "According to the grace of God which was given to me, like a wise master builder I laid a foundation, and another is building on it. But each man must be careful how he builds on it" (v. 10). In context, the obvious meaning of these words, and the purpose of the imagery, is that Paul "laid the foundation" by planting the church in Corinth. That foundation, upon which the church is built, is Jesus Christ (v. 11), which understood within the larger context of the first four chapters means essentially the same thing as what Paul says in 2:2, "For I determined to know nothing among you except Jesus Christ, and Him crucified."

Since Paul pioneered the gospel in Corinth, his work of preaching Jesus Christ laid the foundation for the establishment of the church at Corinth. He, by God's grace, laid that foundation—he planted the church there. Apollos, also serving by God's grace, followed Paul and, in so doing, performed a watering or building function (depending on which of Paul's images you use). In either case, it is God who should be praised and exalted, not the human instruments. Paul's main point is that whoever is currently serving as the builders at Corinth "must be careful how he builds on it" (v. 10).

In verses 12-15 Paul speaks of the final judgment when believers will give an account of their work to God. Because we tend to dislocate this passage from its local church orientation, these verses have often been taken out of context and applied to the lives of individual believers. But the discussion of building materials and judgment grows out of Paul's comments about having laid the foundation of the church and the care people should exercise in building on that foundation. So, the focus of this passage is on the local church more than on the individual believer's life. In other words, this passage is a strong warning to those who, as spiritual leaders at Corinth, were building the church there. Future leaders might be tempted to use human wisdom and power strategies (cf. 1 Cor. 1:18-2:5) and thus try to build the church with wood, hay, and straw (3:12).

In verses 16-17, Paul calls the body of believers at Corinth the temple of God. This is different from the temple imagery used in 6:19 that refers to the body of a believer. Here Paul uses the second person plural pronoun to indicate that the church at Corinth, as a whole, serves as God's temple or dwelling place (cf. Eph. 2:22). When Paul says, "If any man destroys the temple of God," he refers to destroying the church, not the individual believer's body. In context, "destroy[ing] the temple of God" would refer to using inferior building materials, that is, shifting away from the foundation that Paul had laid, Jesus Christ.

Paul's description of his missionary work in Corinth centered on the building of the local church, confirming what we have been saying about the Great Commission's target. And, as Acts confirms, this is not an isolated example. In fact, we can extend the argument beyond the Corinthian correspondence to make the case that the bulk of the New Testament epistles presuppose the organization and function of the local church. Paul's letters to the believers are often directed to the church or churches (cf. 1 Cor. 1:2, 2 Cor. 1:1, Gal. 1:2, 1 Thess. 1:1, 2 Thess. 1:1). They also indicate that spiritual leaders were in place giving leadership and instruction to the church (1 Thess. 5:12, 1 Tim. 5:17, Eph. 4:11, cf. Heb. 13:17), even identifying the offices that serve the church (Phil. 1:1, 1 Tim. 3:1, 8, Titus 1:5, cf. Acts 20:18, 28). And the kind of spiritual life that the New Testament commands demands that believers exercise spiritual gifts and edify each other, presumably in the context of a local church (e.g., 1 Pet. 4:10-11, Col. 3:16).

This church focus should not surprise us, considering what Paul says about the local church in 1 Timothy 3:15: "I write so that you will know how one ought to conduct himself in the household of God, which is the church of the living God, the pillar and support of the truth." This verse comes after very specific instructions about the activities and offices of a local church, making it clear that Paul is not just referring to the universal, invisible church. Specific instructions about prayer (2:1-8), the role of women (2:9-15), and the qualifications of overseers (3:1-7) and deacons (3:8-13) are all intended to help the local church function as the household of God. These instructions are vital because the church is the pillar and support of the truth. This is why the letters from the Lord in Revelation 2-3 express His satisfaction or dissatisfaction with the local church and its membership, not individual believers per se.

The local church is the centerpiece of God's work in this dispensation. It is no wonder, then, that Paul's missionary efforts extended beyond winning the lost to Christ. He aimed at more than converts; he aimed at planting churches.

### *The Fulfillment of the Great Commission*

Finally, for the apostles, church planting was considered the mark of a reached area. In Romans 15:14-29, Paul provides insight into his own understanding of Christ's mission and work. His summary statement is found in verse 16, "to be a minister of Jesus Christ to the Gentiles, ministering as a priest the gospel of God, so that my offering of the Gentiles may become acceptable, sanctified by the Holy Spirit." As we noted earlier (1 Cor. 3:10), Paul grounds his call and commission in the "grace that was given me from God" (v. 15b).

Two statements in this passage offer particular insight into our study. The first is found in verse 19, "so that from Jerusalem and round about as far as Illyricum I have fully preached the gospel of Christ." The second is in verse 23, "but now, with no further place for me in these regions..." The combination of these two, and the context in which they are found, points toward the conclusion that Paul had some way of answering the question, "How do I know when my missionary work here is complete?" In saying that he had "fully preached the gospel of Christ" and there was "no further place for him" in that area, he informed the Romans that he had reached the target of his missionary endeavors in Macedonia and Achaia, and to some degree, in the entire east (Jerusalem round to Illyricum).

What does Paul mean when he uses the words "I have fully preached the gospel of Christ" to describe his missionary work? O'Brien suggests that there are three possible interpretations of these words: 1) an eschatological view—Paul's preaching was the fulfillment of the Old Testament eschatology; 2) a methodical view—the manner in which Paul preached; or 3) an ecclesiastical view—the scope of Paul's mission.[52] Of these, the third not only best fits the language and context of Romans 15, but also it best accounts for the local church orientation we find in Paul's ministry. "Paul not only proclaimed the gospel and, under God, converted men and women. He also founded churches as a necessary element in his missionary task. Conversion to Christ meant incorporation into him, and thus membership within a Christian community."[53]

---

[52] P. T. O'Brien, *Gospel and Mission in the Writings of Paul: An Exegetical and Theological Analysis* (Grand Rapids: Baker, 1995), 39-42. Douglas Moo (*The Epistle to the Romans*, NICNT [Grand Rapids: Eerdmans, 1996], 895) cites a fourth possibility as "Paul may be claiming to have 'filled' (*pleroo*) the regions indicated with the gospel." He concludes, "this assumes without warrant that the object of the verb is not 'gospel' but 'regions' or something of the sort."

[53] Ibid., 42.

Given Paul's strong commitment to the establishment and strengthening of local churches, how could he arrive at the conclusion that he had fulfilled his assignment? Morris sums it up well:

> Since Paul had done no more than preach in a number of the larger cities, this can scarcely mean that he felt that the whole area named had been evangelized. He is saying that he had done what he, the apostle to the Gentiles, was required to do. He had preached in strategic centers throughout the area named and established churches. No doubt there was much still to be done, both by way of preaching to those not yet converted and of building up in the faith of those who had come to believe.[54]

Paul had fulfilled the preaching of the gospel in that he had laid the foundation of Christian faith in the region: disciples of Jesus Christ and churches to equip and strengthen them—the vehicle through which the rest of the region could be reached for Jesus Christ. "A claim to have fully preached the gospel of Christ is understandable in this sense, for Paul's point is that he has finished planting churches where Christ was not named in the area extending from Jerusalem to Illyricum. This hardly means that every village or town heard the gospel."[55]

This interpretation also helps us understand the second phrase, "with no further place for me in these regions" (v. 23). Clearly, if Paul believed that the goal of his missionary work was winning converts, there would be plenty of "further place" for him in those regions. Since thriving churches was his target he could reach a point where his work as a missionary was done. We must understand Paul's words here in light of his statement in verses 20-21, namely, that he aimed to preach where Christ had not been named so as to avoid building on another's foundation. His use of the foundation imagery here is similar to what we found in 1 Corinthians 3:10.

---

[54] Leon Morris, *The Epistle to the Romans*, in PNTC (Grand Rapids: Eerdmans, 1988), 514.

[55] Thomas R. Schreiner, *Romans*, in ECNT (Grand Rapids: Baker, 1998), 770.

Paul's desire to not "build on another man's foundation" means "he does not want to preach that gospel where another person has already planted a church."[56] Of course, this was a general, governing principle of his ministry, not an unbreakable law.[57]

In one sense, the Great Commission will not be fulfilled until every living person has become a disciple of Jesus Christ. But in terms of developing a theology of missions, fulfilling the Great Commission is more than winning disciples for Jesus Christ. It means establishing local assemblies that operate in obedience to the New Testament. So, in a missionary sense, I believe we could argue, based on Paul's words here, that the Great Commission work of the missionary is completed when a foundation of growing, reproducing local churches has been established. Again, O'Brien summarizes it well:

> So, his claim to have "fulfilled the gospel in an arc right up to Illyricum" signified that he had established strong churches in strategic centers of this area, such as Thessalonica, Corinth, and Ephesus. Further evangelistic outreach and the upbuilding of congregations lay in the hands of others. But for the apostle there was no more place for him to work in these regions, and thus he was "free" to go up to Jerusalem and move on to Spain via Rome.[58]

In summary, Church planting must be the target of the Great Commission because 1) it is the necessary context for disciple-making; 2) it is the work Christ is doing in the earth; 3) it is the main activity of the book of Acts; 4) it is the focus of Paul's missionary efforts, letters, and prayers; and 5) it was considered the mark of a reached area. The New Testament leaves no doubt that church planting was important to the apostles and the main target of fulfilling the Great Commission. It must be our target as well. The next section will flesh out how this truth changes the way we practice missions.

---

[56] Ibid.

[57] Moo, 897.

[58] O'Brien, 43.

Although much more could be said about the place of church planting in missionary work, I want to offer a brief survey of what I believe are significant implications for our thinking about missions and missionaries.

## *Implications for Missions*

The principle that the Great Commission cannot be fulfilled without the planting of churches is the great implication! This principle sets the standard of evaluation for all missions work, and that standard contains three important elements: new, indigenous, and reproducing churches.

### New Testament Missions Must Aim to Plant *New* Churches

New Testament missions must aim to plant new churches. Anything short of that falls short of God's plan. While exceptional circumstances might require limiting missions work to only evangelism, such as work in closed countries, exceptions do not change the rule, they prove it. We should do all we can to see disciples made and churches formed. Limitations on reaching the target in certain contexts do not call us to redirect our focus away from the biblical target.

Sadly, it seems that a combination of our American culture's pragmatism and impatience sends us rushing forward to win as many converts as we can as fast as we can. We want instant success rather than committing to the long-term work of the Great Commission. Fuzzy thinking regarding the target at which a missionary is to aim (churches planted, not just converts won) also aggravates the problem. I often wonder how long American churches would be willing to support a missionary in the United States who sent out monthly reports about the number of converts won, yet never established a church. In most cases, we would seriously question such a practice. But, for some reason, we don't think that way when it comes to foreign missions. We are often content with conversion stories and numbers. Is this acceptance grounded in the Bible? Considering the New Testament practice, we have to contend that it is not.

## New Testament Missions Must Aim to Plant New *Indigenous* Churches

While this section will not be a full discussion of the issues of indigenization and contextualization, what we have seen of the pattern in Acts and Romans 15 demands that we address the basic concept. Without, I hope, oversimplifying a complex debate, I will address two basic aspects of indigenization:

First, Churches must be grounded in the culture, rather than transplanted from another. Consider the following explanation of "Indigenous Churches" in the *Evangelical Dictionary of World Missions*:

> The term "indigenous" comes from biology and indicates a plant or animal native to an area. Missiologists adopted the word and used it to refer to churches that reflect the cultural distinctives of their ethnolinguistic group. The missionary effort to plant churches that fit naturally into their environment and to avoid planting churches that replicate Western patterns.[59]

While the current debate on contextualization has become mired in philosophical and sociological concerns well beyond what is necessary, it is safe to say that most recognize the simple sense of not imposing non-moral elements of one culture upon another under the guise of church planting. The call to follow Christ is not equal to a call to leave one's culture and accept another culture, namely, the one that belongs to the missionary. Paul was fully prepared to make non-moral accommodations in his lifestyle based on the culture of those he aimed to reach for Christ (cf. 1 Cor. 9:19-23). He desired for there to be no barriers except for the gospel itself and no offenses to be given except those entailed in the true gospel (cf. 1 Cor. 10:32-33). Sadly, however, American missionaries too often have failed to see the legitimate and necessary distinction between their own cultural forms of church and how the church should look within the culture in which they minister. Paul planted churches that were indigenous to the culture in which they were established.

---

[59] John Mark Terry, "Indigenous Churches" in *EDWM*, 483.

Second, Churches must be planted to become self-governing, self-supporting, and self-propagating. Indigenous, when used in this context, speaks of the determined effort by the missionary to see that the churches planted have established leadership (cf. Acts 14:23, Titus 1:5-9) and are not permanently dependent on external leadership and support.

Here is the key to the problem: Missionaries have too often trained the converts to depend upon them, rather than to take responsibility for themselves. Missionaries may be overprotective; they may unconsciously desire to be the head and have people look to them as the indispensable man; or they may lack of faith in the Holy Spirit to do His work in maturing the converts. But, for whatever reason, the fact remains that weak churches are often the product of the missionaries' wrong approach to their task.[60]
Although Paul exercised apostolic authority over the churches that he planted, he did not establish a pattern of dependence. He recognized and encouraged the self-government of the churches (e.g., 1 Cor. 5:4-5; 6:1-5; 16:3). He did not establish patterns of regular financial support that came from established churches to new churches in other regions. The target was indigenous churches, so they were begun with the three "selfs" in view: self-government, self-propagation, and self-support. Contemporary missions strategy should not deviate from these apostolic goals.

## New Testament Missions Must Aim to Plant New, Indigenous, *Reproducing* Churches

Paul's basic argument that he had "fully preached the gospel of Christ" and that there was "no further place for [him] in these regions" supplies the third element of the standard by which missionary church planting should be evaluated—the churches that have been planted should be equipped for and engaged in church planting within their own region. Paul expected the churches that had been planted from Jerusalem round to Illyricum to pick up the Great Commission mandate and complete it.

---

[60] Hodges, 17.

This concept is inherent in the Great Commission. When Jesus instructs the disciples that they are to teach "them to observe all that I commanded you," that necessarily implies the Great Commission itself. A church has not been fully established until it becomes obedient to the missionary command! Therefore, we could technically say that the true missionary target is not just church planting, but also a self-perpetuating church planting movement. Like Paul, our missionary goal is to lay a foundation for the spread of the gospel and the planting of churches throughout entire regions.

## *Implications for Missionaries*

If the proper goal of missions is church planting that leads to a self-perpetuating church planting movement, then two mandates for missionaries seem to follow:

### The Primary Mandate for Missionaries is to Plant Churches

In the light of all that has been said above about the importance of church planting, it should come as no surprise that, as I understand the Scriptures, all missionary ministry should be intricately connected to the planting of local churches. Church planting is not one of the things that missionaries do—it is *the* thing! Everything else must be subordinated to this goal. Missionaries win people to Christ in order to establish local churches of believers. Missionaries train pastors so they can assume the leadership of planted churches or go out to plant churches themselves.

Given the diversity of ministries that abound on the mission fields of the world, my point may be unsettling to some. Perhaps it should be! Can anyone doubt that missions, as any local church might, can accrue traditional, accepted practices that have lost sight of the biblical mandate? The missionary enterprise, just like the life of any local church, must constantly be evaluated in light of the Bible, not by "what we have always done before." I believe that the enormous challenges and opportunities of fulfilling the Great Commission demand that we be willing to discipline ourselves to think and act biblically. Good intentions channeled in the wrong direction is not pleasing to the Master; obedience to His revealed will is.

## The Secondary Mandate for Missionaries Is to Play a Support Role in Church Planting

Arguing that the primary mandate for missionaries is to plant churches is not the same as arguing that there are not other roles that missionaries can, and sometimes should, play on the mission field. Primary means exactly that. Since the goal of missions is disciple-making that leads to church planting, all missionary work should focus on church planting. Therefore, the primary work of missionaries is to serve as church planters themselves. In many cases there are support roles in the church planting process that need to be filled by missionaries, but these support roles should do exactly that—support church planting, not supplant it!

American Christians often focus on building institutions (e.g. colleges, hospitals, camps), but this focus is not always needed or helpful on the foreign field. The goal of missions is not to reproduce uniquely American institutions—it is to plant churches that can grow and reproduce. Institutions like these should only be developed in order to assist the church-planting goal, and their effectiveness in doing so should be put to the test, not just accepted as fact. Examination of the facts would often lead to the conclusion that much time, energy, and resources have actually been diverted away from church planting to serve Christian organizations that have little to do with church planting. We must, without exception evaluate all missionary activity by its impact on building local churches.

Missionaries on each mission field need to develop and evaluate an overarching strategy according to the goal of planting churches. If a particular support ministry can genuinely help that cause, then pastors and churches will recognize this and support it. For example, there is often a clear need for missionaries to serve as educators to teach and train church planters. The process of indigenization can be helped by the multiplication of national pastors through carefully developed training programs and institutions. But even here there is great danger that indigenization be threatened by an excessive dependence on American missionaries and models of training.

Considering the New Testament target should stir us to rethink the way we are doing missions, including who we will send, and why we send them. As we stand at the front end of the twenty-first century, the sad truth is that some mission fields that should be mission senders are not so primarily because previous generations focused more on converts than planting indigenous, reproducing churches. If the Lord tarries, my hope and prayer is that the same will not be true by the end of this century.

*And thus I aspired to preach the gospel, not where Christ was already named, so that I would not build on another man's foundation.*

Romans 15:20

# 5

# THE TERRITORY OF THE GREAT COMMISSION

Missions has always been a global endeavor—the church in one area's sending out missionaries to proclaim Christ where He is not worshiped around the world. Taking the gospel "to the remotest part of the earth" has been the task of the church since the book of Acts. Yet some contemporary authors have begun to question the practice of sending missionaries to the ends of the earth. Engel and Dyrness, in Changing the Mind of Missions, boldly question such thinking:

> The changed world situation that we have described suggests a new metaphor for understanding missions. It is no longer appropriate to send missionaries and even resources from a dominant center of political or economic influence to some distant and exotic place.[61]

Those words—*it is no longer appropriate*—are strong words and call into question much, if not most, of what is being done by the churches and missionaries of North America. Not only do they call into question the contemporary practice of missions, but they stand as a challenge to much of the current emphasis regarding unreached peoples and frontier missions. Even more striking is the fact that, taken in context, these writers are calling into question the entire

---

[61] James F. Engel and William A. Dyrness, *Changing the Mind of Missions* (Downers Grove, IL: InterVarsity Press, 2000), 49.

foundation of the missionary movement that began with William Carey's departure from Britain for India in 1793.[62]

While I appreciate their desire to challenge the mindset of colonialism, to argue that sending missionaries is no longer appropriate is more than a "new metaphor for understanding missions." Since the basic definition of a missionary is "one who is sent on a mission,"[63] it would seem that their "new metaphor" actually eliminates missions and missionaries. Yet the concept of "being sent on a mission" is biblical and, therefore, still valid. Most see our modern term "missionary" as rooted in the biblical concept of being sent by Jesus Christ to carry out His mission.[64] As we have noted earlier, Jesus did in fact commission His disciples in sending terms, "Peace be with you; as the Father has sent Me, I also send you" (John 20:21, cf. 4:38; 17:18).

The book of Acts records God's call on the first missionaries in the language of sending: "Then, when they had fasted and prayed and laid their hands on them, they sent [Saul and Barnabas] away. So, being sent out by the Holy Spirit, they went down to Seleucia and from there they sailed to Cyprus" (Acts 13:3-4). So, at the heart of missions is the idea of someone, the missionary, being sent on a mission. Engel and Dyrness seem to assume that the need no longer exists for this kind of sending. This conclusion seems driven more by anthropological opinions than the status of Christ's global mission. In other words, they do not believe that the Great Commission has been fulfilled; they believe that Westernized Christianity should no

---

[62] Carey is referred to twice in the pages preceding the quote above.

[63] Since the term missionary never occurs in our English translations, this definition of it, drawn from *The American Heritage Dictionary of the English Language* (840), must suffice.

[64] "The core New Testament meaning clusters around ideas related to sending and or crossing lines, to those being sent, the sent ones—whether messengers or the Twelve, or the others who serve with some kind of apostolic authority or function. The New Testament affirms that the apostolic messenger (the missionary) becomes the person authoritatively sent out by God and the church on a special mission with a special message, with particular focus on the Gentiles/nations" (William David Taylor, "Missionary" in *Evangelical Dictionary of World Missions*, gen. ed. A. Scott Moreau [Grand Rapids: Baker, 2000], 644.).

longer be exported. This conclusion is confirmed by the fact that they refer to missionaries being sent from one Third-World country to another and to the First-World countries.[65]

But the real question that needs to be asked and answered is: "Has the Great Commission been fulfilled?" The command of Jesus Christ was to "make disciples of all the nations." Has this been done yet? Obviously, these questions cannot be answered without more precisely defining what it means to have made disciples of all the nations. Since we have already defined the disciple-making task, what remains here is to understand what Jesus means by "all the nations." This phrase identifies where the disciple making is to take place, or, as the title of this chapter suggests, the territory of the Great Commission.

Before we consider this issue directly, it is important to remind ourselves of the main reason that this question is important. The chapter on the supremacy of God in missions argued that His glory is the fuel and goal of missions. The entire process of training and sending missionaries to the ends of the earth is only justifiable from a God-centered frame of reference. If we measure success in missions by the number of converts, then the costly and lengthy process of recruiting, training, and then sending missionaries to other cultures is highly suspect. But, because God's glory is ultimate, the mission of taking the name of Christ to the nations of the earth is right simply because God commanded us to do so. Because God's glory is ultimate, He has commanded us to gather a people "from every tribe and tongue and people and nation" to worship the Lamb that was slain. Success in missions should be measured by reaching people from all the nations, not just by reaching as many individuals as possible.[66]

---

[65] *Changing the Mind of Missions*, 48-49.

[66] John Piper provides an excellent elaboration of this concept in chapter five of *Let the Nations Be Glad! The Supremacy of God in Missions* (Grand Rapids: Baker, 1993), although I will argue in this chapter for a different understanding of the term "nations" than he advocates.

## *The Global Nature of the Great Commission*

The commission texts recorded for us in Matthew, Mark, Luke, and Acts declare that Christ's will is that the gospel be taken to the ends of the earth.

- Go therefore and make disciples of all the nations, baptizing them in the name of the Father and the Son and the Holy Spirit (Matt. 28:19).
- And He said to them, "Go into all the world and preach the gospel to all creation" (Mark 16:15).
- And that repentance for forgiveness of sins would be proclaimed in His name to all the nations, beginning from Jerusalem (Luke 24:47).
- But you will receive power when the Holy Spirit has come upon you; and you shall be My witnesses both in Jerusalem, and in all Judea and Samaria, and even to the remotest part of the earth (Acts 1:8).

The Apostle Paul's commission is also tied explicitly to the spread of the gospel to the nations of the earth. Acts 9:15-16 records the Lord's plans for him communicated to Ananias, "But the Lord said to him, 'Go, for he is a chosen instrument of Mine, to bear My name before the Gentiles and kings and the sons of Israel; for I will show him how much he must suffer for My name's sake.'" Paul's testimony about the Lord's commission found in Acts 22:21 also emphasizes this fact, "And He said to me, 'Go! For I will send you far away to the Gentiles.'" Paul's distinctive place in God's plan was to be the apostle to the Gentiles (cf. Gal. 1:16; 2:2, 8,9). In each of these cases, the Greek word translated Gentiles is ethnos, which is translated as "nations" in Matthew 28:19.

While some argue that the nation of Israel had a missionary mandate to take the worship of Yahweh to the nations of the earth,[67] the Old Testament provides little basis for this conclusion.

---

[67] E.g., Walter Kaiser, *Mission in the Old Testament: Israel as a Light to the Nations* (Grand Rapids: Baker, 2000), 9-10.

> To contend that Israel had a missionary task and should have engaged in mission as we understand it today goes beyond the evidence. There is no suggestion in the Old Testament that Israel should have engaged in 'cross-cultural' or foreign mission.[68]

It is certainly true that the nations were called to worship the true and living God, but they were to come to God via Israel. Israel was not "sent" to them in any missionary sense. The nations were to come to God; therefore, contrary to Kaiser's view,[69] the emphasis is centripetal, not centrifugal. Historically, the Gentiles could be incorporated into Israel (e.g., Rahab and Ruth), and prophetically, Gentiles will be gathered to Israel during the Kingdom (e.g., Isa. 2:2-4).[70]

The global mission to make disciples is a new work given to the disciples of Jesus Christ on the basis of His death and resurrection. He now has been given "all authority in heaven and on earth" (Matt. 28:18), and that forms the basis of the disciples' commission ("Go therefore"). Since Christ is exalted over all, "God is now declaring to men that all people everywhere should repent" (Acts 17:30). James summarized God's purpose as "taking from among the Gentiles a people for His name" (Acts 15:14). There can be no doubt that the New Testament commands and expects the spread of the gospel to all nations.

## *The Nations of the Great Commission*

While there is little debate about the global nature of the Great Commission, there is considerable debate about how the "all nations" portion of the Commission should be understood. In the last three decades there has been a decided shift in missionary emphasis to focus on unreached peoples rather than unreached

---

[68] Andreas J. Kostenberger and Peter T. O'Brien, *Salvation to the Ends of the Earth: A Biblical Theology of Mission* (Downers Grove, IL: InterVarsity, 2001), 35.

[69] Kaiser, 9.

[70] Kostenberger and O'Brien, 35.

territories.[71] This emphasis on "peoples" rather than countries owes much of its strength to the writings of Donald McGavran, but a pivotal moment of missions thinking came at the Lausanne Congress on World Evangelism in 1974 when Ralph Winter challenged those assembled about the church's blindness to people groups.

> Why is this fact not more widely known? I'm afraid that all our exultation about the fact that every *country* of the world has been penetrated has allowed many to suppose that every *culture* has by now been penetrated. This misunderstanding is a malady so widespread that it deserves a special name. Let us call it "people blindness," that is, blindness to the existence of separate *peoples* within *countries*—a blindness, I might add, which seems more prevalent in the U.S. and among U.S. missionaries than anywhere else.[72]

In one sense, this was a normal and proper refinement of missionary strategy that followed many others that had been made throughout the modern missionary era. Samuel Wilson compares it to the shift in missions that occurred as the missionaries began to recognize the need to penetrate more deeply into the vast regions reached in the first wave of mission activity, and, subsequently, the focus looked to the interior of these great continents. Growing out of this new emphasis were mission agencies like the African Inland Mission, Sudan Interior Mission, and the China Inland Mission.[73] From this perspective, the new emphasis on people groups has sharpened our focus on missions in a very profitable way. It has taken missions thinking to a new level and highlighted the next step in fulfilling the Great Commission.

But in another sense, the focus on people groups has become so intense and unyielding that it may be causing some distortion in missions. Some seem to argue that the only thing legitimately called missions is the effort to reach the unreached people groups of the

---

[71] Piper, 170.

[72] Cited in Piper, 170-171.

[73] Samuel Wilson, "Peoples, People Groups" in *Evangelical Dictionary of World Missions*, 745.

world. Frank Severn is representative of those who are concerned about the potential imbalance of emphasis that has resulted:

> I fear that our desire to reach every people group has led us to conclude that vast areas have been reached, when, in fact, the gospel is not known there, and the church has not penetrated large portions of the population. These areas should also be targets for mission.[74]

The emphasis on people groups quickly narrows its focus to those groups that are labeled as "unreached" and calls God's people to make reaching them the top, if not exclusive, priority of missions. Some even stress reaching "unreached" groups as the key to finally fulfilling the Great Commission. For example, Rankin argues:

> To finish the task, we first must define it. God does not view the world as we view it, that is, as geo-political nations. He sees the world as "people" (ethno-linguistic groups). If you could count how many peoples, tongues, tribes, and nations exist in the world today who are not yet evangelized, you would be moving toward defining the task that remains to be finished.[75]

This emphasis on reached and unreached people groups has, for better or for worse, transformed missiology. Before we can evaluate the relative merits or demerits of this transformation, we must sharpen our definitions of these ideas.

### What is a People Group and When is it Reached?

These simple questions are not easily answered, or at least are not answered consistently in missionary literature. As will be noted below, there are many ways to define a people group, and the concept of reached versus unreached is flexible as well. For our purposes, we will allow one of the key leaders within the movement

---

[74] "Some Thoughts on the Meaning of 'All Nations'", *EMQ* (October 1997), 416.
[75] Jerry Rankin, "The Unfinished Task" in *Missiology*, ed. John Mark Terry, Ebbie Smith, and Justice Anderson, (Nashville: Broadman, 1998), 668.

to supply the definitions for us. As already noted, Ralph Winter is given credit for focusing the attention of the evangelical world on the people group concept. In an article tracing developments in this concept, he recounts that a crucial meeting on unreached peoples held in 1982 supplied the following two definitions:

- A People Group is *"a significantly large grouping of individuals who perceive themselves to have a common affinity for one another because of their shared language, religion, ethnicity, residence, occupation, class or caste, situation, etc. or combinations of these."* For evangelistic purposes it is *"the largest group within which the Gospel can spread as a church planting movement without encountering barriers of understanding or acceptance."*
- An Unreached People Group is *"a people group within which there is no indigenous community of believing Christians able to evangelize this people group."*[76]

While there are further distinctions that can be made within both of these definitions, they can serve well as a working frame of reference to evaluate the concepts.

### Some Concerns About the People Group Emphasis

While it seems clear that the modern concept of nation-state does not fit completely with the realities in the ancient world, the arguments for a focus on unreached people groups (versus unreached territories) need to be examined carefully.

### Anthropology or Theology?

Fundamental to this whole discussion is whether the missiological emphasis on people groups is being derived from the Scriptures or imposed upon it. I believe there is solid evidence that, in most cases, it is the latter.

First, this emphasis originated in the Church Growth Movement and was rooted in its Homogeneous Unit Principle (HUP). Donald McGavran articulated this principle: "people like to become

---

[76] Ralph D. Winter, "Unreached Peoples: Recent Developments in the Concept" in *Mission Frontiers* (September 1989).

Christians without crossing racial, linguistic, or class barriers."[77] Church Growth strategy, therefore, calls for the formation of churches along the lines provided by these shared characteristics (and others). Viewed in relation to missions, HUP demands cross-cultural evangelism and church planting as the only effective means of reaching the various people groups. So the missionary emphasis on *ethne* as people groups seems to have been driven more by Church Growth strategy than Scripture.

Second, the way in which the term "people groups" is defined usually is the product of modern sociology and anthropology, not biblical studies. John Piper is a clear exception to this, but he acknowledges the difference between his approach and that of most missiologists. He writes:

> I agree with those who say that the Biblical concept of "peoples" or "nations" cannot be stretched to include individuals grouped on the basis of things like occupation or residence or handicaps. These are sociological groupings that are very relevant for evangelistic strategy but do not figure into defining the *Biblical* meaning of "people" or "nations."[78]

This clarification is good and needed. Others do not exercise the same kind of care. The Lausanne Movement, a primary catalyst for the emphasis on people groups, has followed McGavran in defining a homogeneous unit as "a section of society in which all members have some characteristic in common." Commenting on this definition, *The Pasadena Statement* drafted under the chairmanship of John Stott states, "Used this way, the term is broad and elastic. To be more precise, the common bond may be geographical, ethnic, linguistic, social, educational, vocational, or economic, or a combination of these and other factors."[79]

---

[77] Donald McGavran, *Understanding Church Growth*, 3rd ed. revised and edited by C. Peter Wagner (Grand Rapids: Eerdmans, 1990), p. 163.

[78] *Let the Nations Be Glad!*, 172.

[79] John Stott, ed., *Making Christ Known: Historic Mission Documents from the Lausanne Movement, 1974-1989* (Grand Rapids: Eerdmans, 1996), 61-62.

Others unhesitatingly include sociological factors into the definition of a people group. Dayton and Fraser argue that people group "refers to people bound together by the same manners, customs, or other distinctive features" and that the Greek word *ethnos* "comes the closest to modern anthropological terms for labeling people groups."[80] The length this term can be stretched is demonstrated in their comments on the meaning of *ethne*.

> The problem is that the English term *nation* has the connotation of a geographically bounded political state. Such a state has many *ethne* in the New Testament sense of the word. This is especially true in the United States, with its Puerto Ricans, southern Blacks, Cantonese-speaking Chinese, Navajo Indians, New England Italian Catholics, Vietnamese refugees, midwestern farmers, and so on.[81]

I find it hard to believe that anyone thinks the biblical concept of ethne can be stretched to include as specific a people group as "midwestern farmers"! The fact that such a group is identified provides evidence that sociology or anthropology too often drives the discussion. We must be careful that we don't impose sociological or anthropological concepts onto the text of Scripture, making the biblical text say something it never meant. It seems quite possible that the word ethne has received the same type of treatment that the Greek word dunamis has received, namely that a later word (dynamite) has been used to elaborate the meaning of the biblical word. The fallacy is that when Paul used dunamis he could not have been thinking "dynamite" since it had not even been invented yet! The question regarding ethne is similar when we press our current meaning of "ethnic" on the biblical word. Are we making it mean more than it did in biblical times?

**The Elusive Definition of People Group**
When the actual discussion of people groups begins, the problem of definition immediately surfaces. As noted above, this is often

---

[80] Edward R. Dayton and David A. Fraser, *Planning Strategies for World Evangelization*, 2nd ed. (Grand Rapids: Eerdmans, 1990), 86.
[81] Ibid., 87.

complicated by the anthropological perspective that dominates the discussion. But even those who restrict themselves to supplying a biblical definition of the concept encounter great difficulty.

The word *ethnos* means "a body of persons united by kinship, culture, and common traditions" or "people groups foreign to a specific people group."[82] It may be used to identify a corporate entity like a nation, as when the Pharisees, in John 11:48, were worried that "the Romans will come and take away our place and our nation (*ethnos*)." Here the Jewish people are viewed as a national entity, a group with geopolitical significance.

It may also be used to represent a group of individuals of non-Jewish descent, that is, Gentiles or pagans. For instance, Paul uses ethne in reference to the Corinthians' unbelieving state when he says they were "pagans" (12:2). This meaning appears to be used when describing those gathered at Cornelius' home. Acts 10:45 records that "All the circumcised believers who came with Peter were amazed, because the gift of the Holy Spirit had been poured out on the Gentiles (ethne) also." This verse is clearly referring to a group of individuals without regard for their status as an ethnic people group (e.g., midwestern farmers!).

An extension of this meaning is an almost technical sense which simply identifies Gentiles as distinguished from Jews and Christians.[83] This is most often translated simply as Gentiles, while it could be translated as nations (as it is in Matthew 28:19). Paul's commission from the Lord is to "bring about the obedience of faith among all the Gentiles" (Rom. 1:5).

The problem is determining if Paul means among the "people groups" or if he is using it in the broad sense (i.e., Gentiles) as most translations suggest. As it stands, there is no reason based on the meaning of the word for forcing the translation "people groups" in

---

[82] BAGD, 276.

[83] "Ethnos" in TDNT, edited by Gerhard Kittle and Gerhard Friedrich, abridged in 1 vol. by Geoffrey W. Bromiley (Grand Rapids: Eerdmans, 1985), 201.

these contexts, nor is there any clear rule for making a decision in this regard. A chief defect of the people group approach is the failure to recognize that simply because a word *can* mean something does not mean it *does* mean that in any particular instance. Even more to the point, they seem guilty of taking a possible meaning and imposing it on most of its uses when, in fact, most translations have not seen this as the case.

The problem of defining *people group* in terms of the missionary task is further complicated by the fact that the Bible also uses other categories to distinguish those who are the object of missions. For example, Revelation 5:9 adds "tribe and tongue and people" to "nation" as the list of those to be reached. If one of the terms used here, nations, can be used in an ironclad way to dictate a group from which believers will be gathered to worship the Lamb, then it seems that the others should be also. But few argue for the others as the basis for missionary strategy.

John Piper does argue strongly that the true biblical target of missions is the "families" or "clans" mentioned in Genesis 12:3, but he has to concede that all attempts at definition must be cautious.

> What we have found, in fact, is that a precise definition is probably not possible to give on the basis of what God has chosen to reveal in the Bible. God probably did not intend for us to use a precise definition of people groups so as to think we could ever stop doing pioneer missionary work just because we conclude that all the groups with our definition have been reached.[84]

The problem may be more straightforward than that. The difficulty in biblical definition may be due to the fact that the modern concept of people groups is foreign to the thinking presented in Scripture. And if the missionary texts use the term simply as "Gentiles" or in the sense of "the nations" as a whole, then the excessive focus on sociologically defined people groups is without basis. The fact is that

---

[84] Piper, 205.

no clear missionary text can decisively be used to prove the sociological definition of this term. It just is not clearly provable.

On a practical level, the final definition of people groups often results in groups too small to fit the methodology of indigenous church planting presented in Scripture. Piper even admits this.[85] This provides part of the explanation for the elaborate systems that have been developed to support the people group approach. Ralph Winter in one place argues for distinguishing between micro, mini, macro, and mega people groups[86] and in another, along with Bruce Koch, speaks of "four useful ways" to speak about people groups: blocs, ethnolinguistic peoples, unimax peoples, and sociopeoples.[87] The sheer complexity of these schemes and discussions provides evidence that this approach is not something drawn from the clear teaching of Scripture.

On the historical and theoretical levels, if the categories of Revelation 5:9 serve as an ironclad paradigm for God's eternal redemptive purpose, how can we account for those people groups or clans that have ceased to exist without hearing the gospel? In other words, if God has purposed to include someone from every people group (as defined above), then He must have saved individuals from the people groups that existed throughout the Old Testament era, and individuals from all of the people groups who existed even apart from the gospel in this dispensation.

Obviously, this raises the question as to how these people could be saved apart from the gospel. Solid evangelicals like Piper refuse to accept the inclusivist positions currently being advocated by some.[88] Additionally, Piper, while acknowledging his belief that infants who die are safe in God's grace, does not allow for this to fulfill the scope of Revelation 5:9.

---

[85] Ibid., 211.

[86] Winter, "Recent Developments"

[87] Ralph D. Winter and Bruce A. Koch, "Finishing the Task: The Unreached Peoples Challenge," *Mission Frontiers* (June 2000), 24-25.

[88] He devotes an entire chapter of *Let the Nations Be Glad!* to defending the necessity of conscious faith in Jesus Christ alone for salvation.

> I do believe that infants who die will be in the kingdom....However God does not ever mention this or relate it in any way to the missionary enterprise or to the promise that all the families of the earth will be blessed. Rather it appears to be his purpose to be glorified through the conversion of people who recognize his beauty and greatness, and come to love him above all gods. God would not be honored so greatly if the only way he got worshippers from all the nations was by the natural mortality of infants.[89]

So, infant mortality cannot account for members of "all the nations" being gathered before the Lamb. Having taken this position, Piper is pressed to alter the emphasis of these texts so that "the meaning of the promise and the command concerning the nations is that 'all the nations' refers to all those who exist at the consummation of the age. When the end comes there will be no existing people group that is left out of the blessing."[90]

This is too convenient an escape from the problem created by forcing the people group concept on top of biblical terms. There is no textual support in Revelation 5 for limiting the group from "every tribe and tongue and people and nation" to only those who exist at the time of Christ's return. In fact, since the scene in Revelation five presents the culmination of the entire church age, it would be proper to assume that those gathered in 5:9 are representative of all the redeemed throughout church history, not just those saved at its end.

I believe there is a much easier answer to this problem, and that is to understand the terms more broadly than the people group emphasis does. That is, allow "nations" to have the meaning in the missionary passages that it clearly has in other texts where the intent is not to identify a specific ethnic group. For example, when Jesus commanded His disciples, "Do not go in the way of the Gentiles, and do not enter any city of the Samaritans; but rather go to the lost sheep of the house of Israel" (Matt. 10:5-6), He was not using *ethnos* in the sense of people groups. He was speaking more broadly than

---

[89] John Piper, 209, footnote 33.
[90] Ibid.

that, and it seems reasonable, even proper, to take His use of the same word in Matthew 28:19 the same way.

Likewise, it would be far less complicated if it was simply acknowledged that Revelation 5:9 uses "every tribe and tongue and people and nation" to stress the global scope of Christ's redemption, not to establish people group categories. While commentators disagree among themselves about the exact significance of each term,[91] they seem to agree that the point of their use is to demonstrate that "Jesus' death secured a salvation universally applied to all classes and peoples of the earth."[92] As Morris notes, "The universal scope of redemption receives mention with the piling up of expressions to show that the redeemed come not from any restricted group but from all over the world."[93] Aune puts it most succinctly, "These lists are meant to emphasize universality."[94] So, rather than establishing missiological units that must be reached in order to fulfill the Great Commission, this text simply demonstrates that Jesus Christ will be worshipped by all peoples.

In spite of all the efforts to study and articulate the definition of a people group, no consistent and biblically justifiable definition has been achieved. We should then be very cautious about building our whole approach to missions on this foundation. There is value in opening our eyes to see that "nations" means more than countries, but the current emphasis seems to go well past what is appropriate and advisable.

---

[91] E.g., Robert L. Thomas (*Revelation 1-7* [Chicago: Moody, 1992], 401) sees a distinction among the terms, while Robert H. Mounce (*The Book of Revelation* [Grand Rapids: Eerdmans, 1977], 148) considers it "fruitless" to attempt such distinctions.

[92] Alan Johnson, "Revelation" in *Expositor's Bible Commentary*, vol. 12, gen. ed. Frank E. Gaebelein (Grand Rapids: Zondervan, 1981), p. 469.

[93] Leon Morris, *Revelation*, TNTC (Grand Rapids: Eerdmans, 1983), p. 99. Walvoord (*The Revelation of Jesus Christ* [Chicago: Moody, 1966], p. 118) also takes these as expressing the "worldwide" work of redemption.

[94] David Aune, *Revelation 1-5*, WBC (Dallas: Word, 1997), p. 362.

## The Issue of Completion

One of the driving forces of the people group emphasis has been the challenge to finally fulfill the Great Commission. In many senses this desire is admirable. It has been a powerful stimulus to move God's people toward missions. But even the foundation of this argument is suspect.

Built on Matthew 24:14 ("This gospel of the kingdom shall be preached in the whole world as a testimony to all the nations, and then the end will come"), the basic argument has been that the gospel must go to all the people groups ("the nations") before the return of Jesus Christ. This view faces some difficulties. To start with, the text is within a prophetic context that is open to debate as to what time period it applies to. Some take it as referring to the time prior to A.D. 70,[95] but more significant for our purposes is the difference between the pre-and post-tribulational views. Those who believe that the Bible teaches a pre-tribulational rapture of the church, understand this text as referring to the gospel proclamation that occurs during the tribulation.[96] Those who hold to the post-tribulational view believe this text refers to this age.[97] My purpose is not to engage in a full discussion of the options, but to point out that this text has a context that must be considered before it is used as a proof text for missions. From pre-tribulational perspective, this is not a text that should be used to define when Christ will come for the church.

But regardless of one's view of the end times, the text itself uses "to all the nations" in combination with "in the whole world" in such a way that moderates the people group emphasis. In fact, when the text says that the gospel "shall be preached in the whole world" it establishes the terminal point ("then the end will come") in geographical, not people group, terms. The measurement, then, is not that someone *from* all the nations will have trusted Christ, but

---

[95] E.g., Craig L. Blomberg, *Matthew* (Nashville: Broadman, 1992), p. 356, and Broadus, *Matthew*, 485.

[96] E.g., Stanley D. Tousaint, *Behold the King: A Study of Matthew* (Portland, OR: Multnomah, 1980), 272.

[97] E.g., Piper, 205, and Carson, 499.

that the gospel has gone into the whole world. Piper acknowledges that the text does not mention anything about the response of the nations to the gospel.[98] Winter, while basing his view of completion on this text, hesitates to make an "inevitable" link between completion of the Great Commission and Christ's return because we cannot be sure our definitions of completion match exactly with God's.[99] In the end, this kind of appeal to Matthew 24:14 lacks the clarity that is needed to make it the watchword of missions.

## The Geographical Focus of the New Testament

Perhaps the greatest concern is how out of step the people group advocates are with the persistent New Testament emphasis on geography. The non-Matthean commission texts all have this focus: "into all the world" (Mark 16:15), "to all the nations, beginning from Jerusalem" (Luke 24:47), "I also have sent them into the world" (John 17:18), and "My witnesses both in Jerusalem, and in all Judea and Samaria, and even to the remotest part of the earth" (Acts 1:8). I would argue that the phrase in Matthew 28:18, "make disciples of all the nations," needs to be understood in light of the other geographically oriented phrases in Matthew: "the field is the world" (13:38), "preached in the whole world" (24:14), and "this gospel is preached in the whole world" (26:13). Whether these verses apply to this dispensation or not is beside the point. They all communicate the significance of geography in Matthew's gospel.

The New Testament record of progress in the missionary endeavor also focuses on geography. Consider how Acts describes it:

- The word of God *kept on spreading*; and the number of the disciples continued to increase greatly *in Jerusalem*, and a great many of the priests were becoming obedient to the faith (6:7).
- Therefore, those who *had been scattered went about* preaching the word (8:4).
- Now when the apostles in Jerusalem heard that *Samaria had received the word* of God, they sent them Peter and John (8:14).

---

[98] *Let the Nations Be Glad!*, 210.
[99] Winter, "Recent Developments."

96

- So, when they had solemnly testified and spoken the word of the Lord, they started back to Jerusalem, and were *preaching the gospel to many villages* of the Samaritans (8:25).
- And the word of the Lord was being *spread through the whole region* (13:49).
- When they had *spoken the word in Perga,* they went *down to Attalia* (14:25).
- After some days Paul said to Barnabas, "Let us return and visit the brethren *in every city in which we proclaimed the word* of the Lord, and see how they are" (15:36).
- They passed *through the Phrygian and Galatian region,* having been forbidden by the Holy Spirit *to speak the word in Asia* (16:6).
- This took place for two years, so that *all who lived in Asia* heard the word of the Lord, both Jews and Greeks (19:10).

My point in highlighting these references is to make sure that we do not miss what we might easily pass over, namely, that the spread of the gospel is pictured as a geographical expansion. That should not surprise us since Acts 1:8 details Christ's commission in geographical terms.

What is true of Acts is also true of Paul when he speaks of his missionary endeavors. When he speaks about the gospel going forth, he uses phrases like "throughout the whole world" (Rom. 1:8), "in all the world" (Col. 1:6), and "in all creation under heaven" (Col. 1:23). He commended the Thessalonians because "the word of the Lord has sounded forth from you, not only in Macedonia and Achaia, but also in every place your faith toward God has gone forth" (1 Thess. 1:8). When he writes of his missionary accomplishments and plans, he uses geography to mark them off:

- In the power of signs and wonders, in the power of the Spirit; so that *from Jerusalem and round about as far as Illyricum* I have fully preached the gospel of Christ (Rom. 15:19).
- But now, with no further place for me *in these regions*, and since I have had for many years a longing to come to you whenever *I go to Spain*—for I hope to see you in passing, and to be helped

on my way there by you, when I have first enjoyed your company for a while (Rom. 15:23-24).

Based on the cumulative weight of these texts, it seems clear that the primary focus of the New Testament is on the geographical expansion of the gospel into all the world, and that the definition of "all the nations" in the Great Commission should be understood in light of this, not vice versa. In fact, Acts 13:47 helps us bring these two ideas into their proper relationship to each other:

> For so the Lord has commanded us, "I have placed you as a light for the Gentiles, that you may bring salvation to the end of the earth."

The word translated "Gentiles" is the same word translated "nations" in the Great Commission, so it could be translated "as a light for the nations." The key here is to note the parallelism between the two lines: being a light for the Gentiles/nations is parallel to bringing salvation to the end of the earth. In other words, even the concept of "nations" is tied to geographical language ("end of the earth").

## Conclusions

I am grateful for the fresh insights into missions that the emphasis on people groups has provided. Positive benefits of this thinking include more deliberate and discerning efforts at indigenization so that missionaries can avoid unnecessary obstacles and offenses. Calling us to look beyond the purely political frame of reference has also awakened us to hidden mission fields among the countries of the earth.

However, those who espouse the people group concept are too optimistic in their view of the Scriptural support for it. There is simply not enough evidence to press this sociological perspective on the Scriptures and make it the standard by which fulfillment of the Great Commission can be measured. The predominant focus of the New Testament is the expansion of the church among the unreached places and peoples of the earth. In fact, I believe that the people group emphasis reads the Great Commission in an imbalanced manner. The focus of the commission is on the verb, "make disciples," not on "of all the nations." The rest of the commission elaborates what it means to make disciples, not who should be made disciples. And the other commission texts clearly confirm this since they all focus on geographical expansion. Since Great Commission focuses on making disciples and it supplies its own terminal point at the end of the age, I would argue that we should not think in terms of fulfilling the Great Commission as if we can get it all done. Christ gave us an assignment to carry out until He returns, and there is no indication that completion of the assignment triggers His return.

I am not sure that there is anything to be gained biblically by targeting specific people groups versus identifying areas where there is no gospel witness and no church planting movement. Paul's burden was "to preach the gospel, not where Christ was already named, so that I would not build on another man's foundation" (Rom. 15:20). Note that he did not say his burden was to find unreached people groups; it was to preach in places where Christ had not been named. Granted, there may be methodological benefits of targeting people groups, but that is an extra-biblical issue that should not be advocated as if it is biblical.

So, whether we view the objective as unreached places or unreached peoples, our burning desire must be to take the gospel to those who have not heard of Christ and among whom there is no viable church planting movement. Current mission work is too heavily tilted in favor of those places where the gospel already has a strong presence. So we must loudly sound the cry for pioneer missionaries to rise up to the challenge of taking the gospel into unreached frontiers! The territory of the Great Commission is global, and the "hot spots" of the battle are those places where Christ has not been named.

We must renew our commitment to make God's purpose for missions ours—where we go is decided by God's agenda to call out a people for His name, not our "bang for the buck" theories! Stated another way, the success of missions should not be measured by the

FOR THE SAKE OF HIS NAME

number of converts, but by the spread of the gospel to all those whom God wants to hear it and by the gathering in of all those whom God wants to worship His Son. Perhaps nothing else reveals more clearly whether our focus is man-centered or God-centered. If we think the ultimate purpose of missions is winning large numbers people to Jesus Christ, it is almost impossible to justify using scarce resources to reach distant, resistant harvest fields when we have near, fertile fields all around us.

In Oklahoma City on April 19, 1995, at 9:02 a.m., a bomb ripped through the Alfred P. Murrah Federal Building causing the deaths of 168 people, including 19 children, and leaving hundreds injured. Suppose we were in the area when the explosion happened, and we immediately ran to the scene to offer help. When we arrive we encounter a section of the building laid open from the blast with dozens of wounded people lying amidst the rubble. We frantically begin to pull people from the wreckage, doing all we can to save as many people as possible. There are five of us struggling to uncover and rescue dozens of people trapped in the rubble—the task is overwhelming.

From around the corner emerges a lone worker who pleads with us to come help him rescue an officemate who is trapped in another part of the building. We quickly ask how many people are trapped with him—he answers that the man is alone. We ask if he is alive and can be rescued quickly—he answers that he does not know. We pause from our frantic rescue work to confront the choice in front of us: do we continue working here where there are already more people to rescue than we can manage, or do we leave these desperate folks in order to attempt the rescue of one man on the other side of the building?

Common sense and pragmatic strategy would argue for staying at the job in front of you. By the time you make it to the spot where the lone man is trapped, you could have rescued two, three, maybe four people in the area where you are already working. If your goal is to rescue as many people as possible, then the choice is clear—stay right there.

The application of this illustration to missions is obvious. If our ultimate purpose is to save as many people as possible, then our attention and resources would be far better spent than seeking out the lost among the unreached peoples of the world or by taking the gospel into cultures that are hardened and resistant to Christ. If reaching more people is the purpose of missions, then our attention should be on receptive peoples, not unreached peoples. The only way to justify leaving a fertile field (e.g., Samaria) to go into a desert to reach one man (e.g., an Ethiopian eunuch) is the will of God. And the will of God, revealed in Scripture, is that God wants the gospel preached to the ends of the earth. He will gather a people "from every tribe and tongue and people and nation" to worship His Son. We must go to the unreached places and peoples because God said so! And God takes priority over strategic considerations, because God, not man, is supreme in missions.

*From there they sailed to Antioch, from which they had been commended to the grace of God for the work that they had accomplished. When they arrived and gathered the church together, they began to report all things that God had done with them and how He had opened a door of faith to the Gentiles.*

Acts 14:26-27

# 6

## THE LOCAL CHURCH'S ROLE IN MISSIONS

My desire in writing this book is to challenge the next generation to reach the world for Christ. More than anything else I want to see God honored by His people's obedience to the Great Commission and the calling out of a people from the nations of the earth for His name's sake. But the majority of Christians in local churches will not end up on a foreign mission field, but instead serve here at home. So far, we have looked at missions mainly from the missionary perspective, but the subject of missions, since it is a biblical subject, should not be limited to those on the foreign field, pastors, and educators. The Great Commission is a universal Christian responsibility. My task in this chapter is to offer a brief survey of topics that are vital to the work of missions in and through the local church.

The topic of this chapter is also important because of the New Testament emphasis on the local church. Missions cannot be properly addressed apart from the context of the local church. Individual believers engage in missions, but I would contend that they must do so in connection with the local church. Each local church will be accountable for how they obey the Scriptures, so we must give energy to understanding how to apply them to the church's missions program. Both our pragmatic culture and church tradition often fight against thinking biblically, so we must work to hold ourselves accountable to the Scriptures. If we look to the Bible for insight and instruction about the local church's role in world missions, we can summarize its teaching in four key words: supplication, sending, supervision, and support.

## *The Local Church Must Pray for Missionaries*

Prayer is an essential element of the believer's life (1 Thess. 5:17) and a crucial part of life in the local church (1 Tim. 2:1). The New Testament is full of prayers and requests to pray for the spread of the gospel. However, this is an element that is sorely neglected in our prayer meetings where requests for health and physical well-being often dominate. While we should pray for the health and physical needs of fellow believers (Jas. 5:13-18), we should carefully consider the emphasis of the New Testament and resolve to pray for missions in three specific areas: the supply of missionaries, the success of the missions message, and the safety of missionaries.

### *Prayer for the Supply of Missionaries*

First, we should be praying for God to raise up and send out missionaries. The biblical basis for this prayer focus is Matthew 9:36-38:

> Seeing the people, He felt compassion for them, because they were distressed and dispirited like sheep without a shepherd. Then He said to His disciples, "The harvest is plentiful, but the workers are few. Therefore beseech the Lord of the harvest to send out workers into His harvest."

The familiarity of this text should not blind us to its importance regarding our prayer life. We'll break down the text and its implications into two parts: the incentives to pray and the command to pray.

### The Incentives to Pray (vv. 36-37)
Verses 36-37 offer three incentives for prayer. When looking out at the multitudes, the Lord "felt compassion on them." The word translated "compassion" communicates a very strong feeling of empathy. As a verb, it is only used of or by Jesus in the New

Testament.[100] Matthew explains that the Lord felt this strong compassion because of three realities: the seriousness of the problem, the size of the harvest, and the shortage of laborers. We can find our motivation to pray in these same realities.

### *The Seriousness of the Problem*

The Lord was moved with compassion by the seriousness of the problems He observed as He looked out on the multitudes. What did He see? First, He saw the condition of the people, "they were distressed and dispirited" (v. 36). This phrase offers two picturesque descriptions of the people. The first, "distressed" meant originally to skin or flay something and came to be used for any kind of trouble,[101] particularly one involving bullying or oppression.[102] The second, "dispirited," meant literally to be thrown down, and came to mean to be downcast. Broadus writes of this word that it means, "lying down, as being worn out and unable to go forward, or might mean cast off, neglected."[103] Jesus saw a people beaten down and oppressed—both by an oppressive Roman government but more importantly by their bondage to sin and Satan—and he felt strongly compassionate toward them.

Second, the words, "like sheep without a shepherd," indicate that Jesus also saw the failure of Israel's spiritual leaders. The people should have had good guidance, but instead they were like shepherd-less sheep wandering the hillsides. Instead of enjoying a shepherd's care and guidance, they were wandering distressed and downcast. Perhaps worse, their shepherds were actually false guides and hireling shepherds (cf. Zech. 10:2-3; 11:16-17).

There is an amazing parallel here between how Jesus saw the people and how Moses feared that the people of his day would be. In

---

[100] R. T. France, *Matthew* (Grand Rapids: Eerdmans, 1985), 175.

[101] Leon Morris, *The Gospel According to Matthew* (Grand Rapids: Eerdmans, 1992), 239.

[102] D. A. Carson, "Matthew" in *The Expositor's Bible Commentary*, v. 8, gen. ed. Frank E. Gaebelein (Grand Rapids: Zondervan, 1984), 235.

[103] John Broadus, *Matthew* (Valley Forge: Judson Press, 1886), 211.

Numbers 27:16-17, Moses expressed his concern about Israel to the Lord:

> "May the LORD, the God of the spirits of all flesh, appoint a man over the congregation, who will go out and come in before them, and who will lead them out and bring them in, so that the congregation of the LORD will not be like sheep which have no shepherd."

Both Moses and the Lord Jesus were concerned about sheep without a shepherd. As Leon Morris observed, "Goats manage well by themselves, but sheep do not. Sheep without a shepherd points to a people who are in great danger and without the resources to escape from it."[104] Their religious leaders were not leading them to the truth that would set them free. Today there are millions of people who have never heard the name of Christ in unreached areas all across the globe. Jesus, in his compassion, has urged us to pray for them because without Him, they will die in their sins.

### The Size of the Harvest

With the words "the harvest is plentiful" Jesus shifts metaphors from flock to farm and in so doing envisions a vast crop in need of harvesting. Jesus is trying to spread His concern and compassion to His disciples by pointing out the immensity of the task in front of them. One can only imagine how Jesus would respond were He to look out over the far greater population of modern cities and mega-cities. While estimates vary, Patrick Johnstone communicates something of the immensity of the harvest field:

> Depending on the strictness of the criteria used, we estimate that between 15% and 25% of the world's population is beyond the reach of the present proclamation of the gospel. This means that between 800 million and 1,300 million people still need to be given their first opportunity to respond to the gospel.[105]

---

[104] *Matthew*, 239.

[105] Patrick Johnstone, *Operation World* (Grand Rapids: Zondervan, 1993), 27.

How can we see the size of this harvest and not be motivated to pray for about it?

### *The Shortage of Workers*
Though the harvest is plentiful, Jesus points out that "the workers are few." There are not enough people to bring in the harvest, and without harvesters the crop will not be gathered in. The real point here is that Jesus and His disciples were not sufficient to reach the whole harvest. The harvest field is bigger than the work force.

While I believe strongly in the supremacy of God in salvation, we should never ignore biblical statements like this by philosophical conjectures about the impossibility of failing to harvest the elect. Here, as in Romans 10:13-17, there is a clear statement that we have a responsibility to carry out the divine plan. We will never figure out how all this works out, but we do know what has been revealed, and that is what we are accountable to obey. We must pray for God to send more laborers.

### The Command to Pray (v. 38)
In light of the incentives presented in verses 36-37, we should not be surprised that Jesus commands us to pray. In doing so, He uses a word ("beseech") that speaks of the kind of prayer that grows out of a sense of need. We will not pray like this unless we feel the compassion that Jesus felt and sense the burden that was on Him and is on us to reach these people.

But we cannot reach people through our own efforts. We must depend on God, "the Lord of the harvest," to reach the people in "His harvest." God is sovereign over the harvest and we are absolutely dependent on Him to see the task accomplished. God has designed it this way. We must fall at His feet and seek his face about how to reach the harvest. God is bigger than the harvest and demands glory through and from it. J. Hudson Taylor saw this to be true in his experience of seeking workers for the harvest. Due to an accidental fall, he found himself confined to bed with an ever-increasing paralysis that culminated in his being unable to even hold a pen. As the call of China and the challenge of new provinces stood before him, he could do nothing but pray—but what great things could he do through prayer! In answer to prayer God not only raised up a team of pioneer missionaries to take the gospel into the nine unevangelized provinces of China, but He provided the funds to take them there. Here is Taylor's view of his illness:

> Had I been well and able to move about, some might have thought that my urgent appeals, rather than God's working, had sent the eighteen men to China. But utterly laid aside, able only to dictate a request for prayer, the answer to our prayers was more apparent.[106]

The goal of our prayer is very specific, "to send out workers into His harvest." In light of the size of the harvest and shortage of workers, the disciples of Jesus Christ must do something, but contrary to our natural impulse (to work harder), Jesus commands us to pray for more workers. If we are serious about the harvest, we will earnestly beg for God to supply more missionaries to work in it.

### *Prayer for the Success of the Missionary Message*

"Finally, brethren, pray for us that the word of the Lord will spread rapidly and be glorified, just as it did also with you." 2 Thessalonians 3:1 is an often-quoted missionary text, and rightly so. This verse provides powerful hope of a dynamic work of God through the ministry of the Word. The phrase "the word of the Lord" is probably best viewed as the Gospel primarily, but it cannot be separated from the rest of God's revealed truth (cf. Acts 20:27). This is language that reflects the summary statements in Acts of the church's advance (4:29, 31; 6:7; 12:24; 19:20). The spread of the gospel is the spread of the Word, whether called "the word of Christ" (Rom. 10:17), "the word of reconciliation" (2 Cor. 5:19), or "the word of God" (1 Thess. 2:13).

This verse serves as a good reminder that the front line of God's work in this dispensation is the preaching of God's Word. Other activities have their place, but they cannot have first place. God has chosen

---

[106] Howard and Geraldine Taylor, *Hudson Taylor's Spiritual Secret*, rev. and ed. by Greg Lewis (Grand Rapids: Discovery House, 1990), 228.

the "foolishness" of preaching to save the lost. Much of contemporary ministry philosophy seems to have lost its confidence in the effectiveness of God's Word to convert the lost and to conform the saved into the image of Jesus Christ. Any lack of powerful effectiveness is not due to a shortage of power on God's part or any weakness of the Word. It may, however, be evidence of our lack of faith and our lack of prayer.

Paul's desire to see the "word spread rapidly and be glorified" means that he wants it to swiftly advance in its mission. The apostle regularly requested prayer for the progress of the gospel (cf. Eph. 6:19, 20; Col. 4:3, 4). The word translated "spread rapidly" is used in Greek Old Testament of a warrior running in battle. If the Word is to obtain its victory, then prayer is essential because 1) the devil has blinded the minds of unbelievers (2 Cor. 4:4) and has taken them captive (2 Tim. 2:25-26); and 2) the Word will have no impact without the work of the Spirit's enlightening the eyes of those who hear it (1 Cor. 2:14). We must seek the Lord for His gracious work through the Spirit to empower the Word and redeem the lost.

When unbelievers see and accept the truth of God's Word, it is glorified, that is, honored and admired for its inherent worth as the Word of the living God. By calling them to pray for the same thing that happened among them ("just as it did also with you"), Paul helps us understand what it means for the Word to be glorified. In 1 Thessalonians 2:13, he writes:

> For this reason we also constantly thank God that when you received the word of God which you heard from us, you accepted it not as the word of men, but for what it really is, the word of God, which also performs its work in you who believe.

The Word is glorified when it is received for what it is, the word of God, not the word of men. So Paul calls on these Thessalonians to pray for God to do that same kind of work in Paul's other missionary works. The church at Thessalonica was a model church established in a relatively short period of time, and Paul asks believers to pray for other churches to have the same success. Here is a pattern that all churches should embrace as we pray for the work of missionaries around the world. We should pray fervently that the Word would be proclaimed powerfully, and sinners would be saved so that the Word spreads rapidly and is glorified. We should pray for the supply of missionaries and we must pray for the spread of the message.

## Prayer for the Safety of the Missionaries

After Paul requests prayer for his missionary success, he also calls on the Thessalonians to pray for his safety. In 2 Thessalonians 3:2 we find these words, pray for us "that we will be rescued from perverse and evil men; for not all have faith." Paul's ministry was constantly under attack from those who opposed him and the gospel. His life was often threatened and in danger due to their persecutions, so Paul urged his fellow believers to pray that he would be rescued from them. He made the same kind of request of the Romans about his journey to Jerusalem (Rom. 15:31). Acts 21:30-23:33 records God's answers to the prayer requests given by Paul to the Thessalonians and Romans. In answer to prayer, God rescues Paul from the mob (Acts 21:31-32), from the Sanhedrin (Acts 23:10), and has Paul's nephew overhear a plot against Paul's life (Acts 23:16).

There is a mysterious element to God's work in this area. He has chosen prayer as a means by which He delivers and protects. God has often directed people to pray specifically for some servant who is undergoing a trial or hardship unknown to the ones praying. What we can be sure of is that God wants us to pray for those who serve Him on the front lines of the gospel because they are engaging in spiritual warfare and they have very real enemies that oppose them.

The local church must be actively involved in missionary prayer. This is the power supply of the work done on the field.

## The Local Church Must Send out Missionaries

Acts 13:1-4 is a crucial passage for understanding the local church's role in world missions. In recounting for us what God was doing in and through the church at Antioch, we find the pattern of New

Testament missions unfolded at its inception. This passage provides the very delicate and needed balance of the divine and human aspects of sending out missionaries:

> Now there were at Antioch, in the church that was there, prophets and teachers; Barnabas, and Simeon who was called Niger, and Lucius of Cyrene, and Manaen who had been brought up with Herod the tetrarch and Saul. While they were ministering to the Lord and fasting, the Holy Spirit said, "Set apart for Me Barnabas and Saul for the work to which I have called them." Then when they had fasted and prayed and laid their hands on them, they sent them away. So, being sent out by the Holy Spirit, they went down to Selucia and from there they sailed to Cyprus.

### God is the Supreme Agent in the Sending out of Missionaries (vv. 2, 4)

God's Spirit is the ultimate agent in calling out missionaries. The Spirit is the one who called the church to set apart Saul and Barnabas for the work of missions and the Spirit is the one who sent them out. This is why we must pray to the Lord of the Harvest to send workers into His harvest! Our zeal to see people head to the fields of the earth can never run ahead of God's. In the chapter on the missionary call, I describe God's special work in the life of those He desires to serve Him vocationally, including missionaries. Though this passage has some dissimilarities from our day (e.g., the presence of special revelation), it does illustrate the principle that God is sending out laborers into the harvest. God works in the life of a believer to provide both godly ambitions and the abilities necessary to carry them out.

### The Local Church is the Mediating Agent in the Sending out of Missionaries (v. 3)

But we cannot ignore the fact that this passage also says that Saul and Barnabas were set apart *by the church at Antioch* with fasting, prayer, and the laying on of hands. And when they departed on their first missionary journey, the text says that "they [the church at

Antioch] sent them away." God is certainly the ultimate agent in the sending process, but He works through the local church. In this sense, the church serves as a mediating agent in the sending process. In other words, it is the church that confirms the call of God and consecrates missionaries for their task.

That the church must be involved in sending out missionaries should come as no surprise. The local church is both the target and the agent of the Great Commission. Missions springs from the local church and aims to plant local churches because the local church is the centerpiece of God's work in this dispensation (1 Tim. 3:15). The Scriptures also teach about the autonomy of the local church, namely, that it is a self-governing body. No person, except the Lord Himself, or organization outside of the local church can dictate the actions or direct the affairs of the local assembly. Therefore, we should see mission boards as implementing agencies, not sending agencies. Mission boards exist to serve the local church, not vice versa. Mission boards cannot replace the work of the local church in the task of appointing and sending missionaries.

## *The Local Church Must Supervise Missionaries*

Acts 14:26-28 reveals that the apostolic pattern was for missionaries to report back to those who had commended them to the grace of God for the work:

> From there they sailed to Antioch, from which they had been commended to the grace of God for the work that they had accomplished. When they had arrived and gathered the church together, they began to report all things that God had done with them and how He had opened a door of faith to the Gentiles. And they spent a long time with the disciples.

Since they had been set apart by the church at Antioch, it was to the church that they gave their report and accounting of what God had done in and through them. The primacy of the local church as the pillar and support of the truth in this dispensation means that it carries the burden of preserving and perpetuating biblical Christianity (1 Tim. 3:15). Therefore, we must remember that the local church has the primary responsibility for assisting missionaries and exercising loving accountability for the actions and ministry of its missionaries. Too often the responsibility for accountability gets tossed back and forth between the local church and the mission board, or, in some more radical cases, the missionary claims to be accountable only to God. While a missionary should not have his hands tied so that he cannot do the work, missionaries whose lives and ministries are unaccountable to fellow believers are ripe for trouble and out of step with God's Word (cf. 1 Tim. 5:19-21; Heb. 13:17).

## The Local Church Must Support Missionaries

Though seldom considered, 3 John 5-8 provides some profitable principles for missionary support:

> Beloved, you are acting faithfully in whatever you accomplish for the brethren, and especially when they are strangers; and they have testified to your love before the church. You will do well to send them on their way in a manner worthy of God. For they went out for the sake of the Name, accepting nothing from the Gentiles. Therefore we ought to support such men, so that we may be fellow workers with the truth.

### The Reasons to Support Missionaries

Verse 7 provides us with two reasons for missionary support. The first is seen in the missionary's purpose, "they went out for the sake of the Name." "They were not individuals engaged in private business pursuits, but men who had initiated their journey in order to further the cause of 'the Name.'"[107] They "went out" in the same way that Acts 15:40 records Paul's departure for his second missionary journey.[108] "The Name" most certainly is the name of

---

[107] D. Edmond Hiebert, *The Epistles of John* (Greenville, SC: Bob Jones University Press, 1991), 332.

[108] John R. W. Stott, *The Letters of John*, rev. ed. (Grand Rapids: Eerdmans, 1988), 226.

Jesus, and serves as shorthand for both their motive (His glory) and their message (Christ Himself). Two texts from Acts demonstrate "the Name" functions in these ways:

- So they went on their way from the presence of the Council, rejoicing that they had been considered worthy to suffer shame *for His name* (Acts 5:41).
- And there is salvation in no one else; for there is *no other name* under heaven that has been given among men by which we must be saved (Acts 4:12).

The second reason for supporting missionaries is found in the words, "accepting nothing from the Gentiles" (v. 7). Going out for the sake of Christ's name meant going out to bear witness to Him; and for the gospel's sake they would not make themselves dependent on unbelieving Gentiles for support. Though the text does not provide an explicit reason for this choice, there seems to be a connection with Paul's missionary practice detailed in 1 Corinthians 9. Stott summarizes this position well:

> What is here said is that these itinerant evangelists would not (as a matter of policy) seek their support from unbelievers and did not (as a matter of fact) receive their support from them. Christian missionaries were not like many wandering non-Christian teachers of those days (or even the begging friars of the Middle Ages), who made a living out of their vagrancy....Christian ministers and teachers certainly have the right to be supported by those who benefit from their service, as Paul several times insisted (especially in 1 Cor. 9:1-18; Gal. 6:6; 1 Tim. 5:17-18). But a Christian congregation supporting its minister is one thing; missionaries begging money from unbelievers is another.[109]

Local churches should support missionaries who have gone out for *the sake of His Name* so that there will be no hindrance to the gospel message proclaimed by the missionary.

---

[109] Ibid., 226-227.

## The Method of Supporting Missionaries

This passage also provides us with insight into the responsibility we have in supporting missionaries; we are "to send them on their way in a manner worthy of God" (v. 6). These words indicate both what we are to do ("send them on their way") and how we are to do it ("in a manner worthy of God"). "Sending the missionaries on their way involved providing for their journey—supplying them with food and money to pay for their expenses, washing their clothes, and generally helping them to travel as comfortably as possible."[110] Since there are varying levels at which believers could fulfill this responsibility, John calls for it to be done "in a manner worthy of God." The basic idea of this phrase is that we should treat these servants of God in the same way that we would treat God Himself.[111]

## The Result of Supporting Missionaries

The final principle of missionary support in this passage is the result that it accomplishes, "so that we may be fellow workers with the truth" (v. 8). When we engage in missionary support, we actually become a co-laborer in the missionary endeavor. This is what Paul had said about the Philippians:

• In view of your participation in the gospel from the first day until now (Phil. 1:5).
• You yourselves also know, Philippians, that at the first preaching of the gospel, after I left Macedonia, no church shared with me in the matter of giving and receiving but you alone; for even in Thessalonica you sent a gift more than once for my needs (Phil. 4:15-16).

Though we may not all be called to go out *for the sake of His name*, we all should be using the resources that God has entrusted to us for the

---

[110] I. Howard Marshall, *The Epistles of John* (Grand Rapids: Eerdmans, 1978), 85-86.
[111] Glenn W. Barker, "3 John" in *The Expositor's Bible Commentary*, vol. 12, gen. ed. Frank E. Gaebelein (Grand Rapids: Zondervan, 1981), 373.

purpose of seeing His name magnified through those who have gone out.

## *Conclusion*

Two strong practical objectives have motivated the writing of this book: 1) that God will raise up a new generation of missionaries to take the name of Jesus Christ to the unreached places and peoples of the earth; and 2) that every believing member of the next generation will accept his or her role in seeing the Great Commission carried out, whether that means going or staying. The first objective is somewhat dependent on the second for its fulfillment—unless there are godly, dedicated believers who are fully committed to their local churches, then missionaries will not be prayed for, sent out, supervised well, or supported properly.

I hope you will seriously consider God's call on your life and seek to determine if He wants you to carry the gospel to those who have not heard His name. But I also want to urge you not to disobey His commands about every believer's life as it relates to missions. You must pray for the full scope of missionary needs—their supply, success, and safety. You, as a part of the local church, should take seriously the responsibility to send out missionaries and provide them with support, and loving and beneficial accountability. And you should give generously of your resources to support those who have dedicated their lives to going out among the Gentiles *for the sake of His name.*

*How then will they call on Him in whom they have not believed? How will they believe in Him whom they have not heard? And how will they hear without a preacher? How will they preach unless they are sent? Just as it is written, "How beautiful are the feet of those who bring good news of good things!"*

Romans 10:14-15

# 7

# THE CALL TO MISSIONS

Up to this point, we have been laying a philosophical foundation for missions, but now it is time to get personal. To talk about missions in theory is relatively easy and comfortable, but the biblical "theory" of missions cannot truly be discussed without asking the penetrating question, "Why aren't more believers going?" Sadly, we are not the only ones who have asked this question. During his ministry in China, Hudson Taylor encountered this same question.[112]

> A man named Mr. Ni, a cotton merchant and an ex-Buddhist leader, was converted under Hudson Taylor's ministry. Mr. Ni had spent much of his time and money in service to "the gods," yet he was not satisfied by the religions he had studied and taught to others. Then passing an open door on the street one evening, he heard a bell being rung and saw people assembling as if for a meeting. Learning that it was a hall for the discussion of religious matters, he too went in. Leading the meeting was a young foreigner dressed in Chinese garb and speaking and reading quite well in the Ning-po dialect. Mr. Ni could make out every word that was read, but he did not understand them—what was their meaning?
>
> Taylor was teaching about Christ being lifted up like the serpent in the wilderness. Mr. Ni was puzzled and moved by

---

[112] Taylor, *Hudson Taylor's Spiritual Secret*, 97-98.

what he heard. Saved, not condemned? A way to find everlasting life? A God who loved the world? The meeting came to a close. The foreign teacher ceased speaking. And with the instinct of one accustomed to lead in such matters, Ni rose in his place, looked at the audience, and said simply:

"I have long sought for the Truth, but without finding it. I have travelled far and near, but have never searched it out. In Confucianism, Buddhism, Taoism, I have found no rest. But I do find rest in what we have heard tonight. Henceforth I am a believer in Jesus Christ."

This new believer became an ardent student of the Bible. His rapid spiritual growth served as a great encouragement to the Taylors. He emerged as an aggressive soulwinner and leader among the Chinese. One day, when talking with his missionary friend, Mr. Ni raised the question, "How long have you had the Glad Tidings in your country?"

"Some hundreds of years" Hudson replied. "What? Hundreds of years? My father sought the Truth," he continued sadly "and died without finding it. Oh why did you not come sooner?"

This is a probing and penetrating question that demands an answer. Why is it that we in the West have so long enjoyed the blessings of the gospel while there are billions who are lost in darkness and sin?

## *Two Perspectives on the Progress of Missions*

Although we might be quick to offer answers here, we should be careful to answer biblically, and that requires looking at this from both the God-ward and man-ward perspectives.

### *The God-ward Perspective*

From a God-ward perspective we must be careful to answer this question in a way that guards both God's right to rule and His goodness. By His right to rule, I mean the fact that God rules over the affairs of men in such a way that history is under His control, and the progress of missions is clearly a part of history. While Bible-believing people have come to differing conclusions about the extent of God's sovereignty, it seems that biblical faith demands that we confess that the "king's heart is like channels of water in the hand of the LORD; He turns it wherever He wishes" (Pro. 21:1). If this is true, and it is, that certainly has implications regarding the spread of the gospel, the concept of restricted access countries, and a host of other missions-related issues.

A clear illustration of God's sovereignty over the task of missions is found in the ministry of the Lord Jesus Christ. In Matthew 10:5-6 we find Him giving an unusual commission to His disciples: "These twelve Jesus sent out after instructing them: 'Do not go in the way of the Gentiles, and do not enter any city of the Samaritans; but rather go to the lost sheep of the house of Israel.'" Of course, this was a temporary command from the Lord about the Gentile mission, but it provides a clear basis for recognizing that God has the right to direct the timing and scope of the missions mandate. In fact, all of Old Testament history provides proof of this principle.

Sadly, some in our day seem determined to think that such sovereignty is somehow unjust or unfair. If God could have done something about the condition of the lost who have not heard, He certainly would have done it. And, if He could have and did not do it, then God is unjust. In fact, William Carey, who has been called the father of the modern missionary movement, encountered such an attitude from a Brahmin in response to Carey's attacks upon idolatry and false gods.[113] As Carey pressed home Paul's message to the Athenians of repentance over their idolatry (cf. Acts 17), the Brahmin objected that it is God who should repent for not having sent them the gospel sooner.

What does one say to such an objection? Should we tell this worshipper of false gods that the True and Living God really wanted to send the gospel but He couldn't find anyone who would obey Him? In other words, call this pagan to turn in faith to a God whose followers do not follow! But that is not how Carey responded.

---

[113] Tom Wells, *A Vision for Missions* (Carlisle, PA: Banner of Truth, 1985) 12-13.

Instead he pressed the battle with the Brahmin and asserted God's rights as the sovereign Creator. In essence, Carey argued that God could have had He chosen to do so, but He did not do so for reasons based on the good pleasure of His own will (cf. Eph. 1:11).

I can hear the objections already. How could William Carey say such things about God? The answer, quite bluntly, is that Carey knew what the Bible teaches about God more thoroughly than our man-centered world does! He was simply pressing home the truth of Paul's message to the Athenians: "Therefore having overlooked the times of ignorance, God is now declaring to men that all people everywhere should repent" (Acts 17:30). Don't miss the significance of the simple words, "God is now." In other words, Paul is declaring that God is now, after the exaltation of Jesus Christ, engaged in this global ("all people everywhere") evangelistic mission ("should repent"). This is a new phase of God's dealings with humanity, which implies there was a time before this in which God was doing something different. It was God's actions in that earlier time that Carey was rightly defending.

When looking at this from the God-ward perspective, we must guard not only God's right to rule, but His goodness. The man-centeredness of our day causes us to question whether those two can exist together—can God be a sovereign ruler and unqualifiedly good? He can because the Scriptures teach both. We should never question God's goodness, even if He withholds the gospel from nations, because He has righteous reasons for doing so. The Apostle Paul also provides the answer to this question. Preaching to the pagans at Lystra, Paul urges them to turn from their idolatries with these words:

> "Men, why are you doing these things? We are also men of the same nature as you, and preach the gospel to you that you should turn from these vain things to a living God, *who made the heaven and the earth and the sea and all that is in them.* In the generations gone by He permitted all the nations to go their own ways; and yet He did not leave Himself without witness, in that He did good and gave you rains from heaven

and fruitful seasons, satisfying your hearts with food and gladness" (Acts 14:15-17).

Here we find our two issues: God's sovereignty ("He permitted all the nations to go their own ways") and God's goodness ("yet He did not leave Himself without a witness"). Regardless of what God does with regard to the evangelization of the nations, he is still good because man is always accountable for rejecting Him. Paul argues here and in Romans 1 that the pagans have always had a sufficient witness to God's existence:

> For the wrath of God is revealed from heaven against all ungodliness and unrighteousness of men who suppress the truth in unrighteousness, because that which is known about God is evident within them; for God made it evident to them. For since the creation of the world His invisible attributes, His eternal power and divine nature, have been clearly seen, being understood through what has been made, so that they are without excuse. For even though they knew God, they did not honor Him as God or give thanks, but they became futile in their speculations, and their foolish heart was darkened (Rom. 1:18-21).

God has provided a clear revelation of Himself to all people, but mankind has rejected His revelation, leaving them "without excuse" (v. 20). So God not only has the right to govern the progress of missions according to His own purposes, but He is right in all of His dealings with mankind. Any and all who are lost eternally are so because of their own sinfulness and because they have rejected the witness of Him given through general revelation. If God permits some of the nations to sit in darkness in terms of gospel preaching, it does not mean that He has left "Himself without a witness" (Acts 14:17).

### The Man-ward Perspective

However, most of us recognize that the real issue at stake in the fulfillment of the Great Commission is on the man-ward side of the equation. From a man-ward perspective, we must acknowledge that

God has given us the responsibility to take the message of Christ to the ends of the earth. God has chosen to use people as the means by which He will carry out this work. In fact, according to Romans 10:13-17, this is the exclusive means God will use:

> For "Whoever will call on the name of the Lord will be saved." How then will they call on Him in whom they have not believed? How will they believe in Him whom they have not heard? And how will they hear without a preacher? *How will they preach unless they are sent?* Just as it is written, "How beautiful are the feet of those who bring good news of good things!" However, they did not all heed the good news; for Isaiah says, "Lord, who has believed our report?" So faith comes from hearing, and hearing by the word of Christ.

The key portion of this passage for our consideration is found in verse 15, "How will they preach unless they are sent?" The logic of the text is clear: Salvation is granted to all who call on the Lord. But people cannot call on the Lord if they do not believe in Him. They cannot believe in Him if they do not hear the word that proclaims Christ. And that word will not be heard unless someone preaches it. But a preacher is nothing more than a herald, a person entrusted by another with a message. Thus preaching, finally, cannot transpire unless someone sends the preachers.[114]

This text stresses two things. First, it makes absolutely clear the need for the gospel message to be taken in order for people to come to Christ. Contrary to what some are teaching, there is no way to God except through explicit faith in Jesus Christ. Second, it teaches that the message is carried by those who are sent. But we need to ask, "Sent by whom?" And the obvious answer to that question seems to be, "Sent by God." As one commentator aptly notes, "The point of the fourth question is that true Christian preaching, through which Christ Himself speaks, is not something which men can accomplish

---

[114] Douglas J. Moo, *The Epistle to the Romans*, NICNT (Grand Rapids: Eerdmans, 1996), 663.

on their own initiative: it can only take place where men are authorized and commissioned by God."[115]

While I recognize that the issue of a missionary call has often been debated, and the debate itself has often been quite confusing, I am not comfortable with the position that a call is unnecessary. In this regard, I take a somewhat different position than those who were at the center of the Student Volunteer Movement. They argued very strongly that every Christian should go to the mission field unless clearly directed by God to do something else, and that no "special call" from God was needed to enter the missionary endeavor.[116] Based on the text above and others like it, I believe that God does work in a special way to direct servants to the mission fields of the world.

## *Clarifying the Call to Missions*

One of my greatest frustrations as a youth pastor came in connection with this issue. It seemed that everyone talked about "the call to ministry" or "the call to missions" without ever clarifying what they meant by those words. In fact, the basis for using them was too often grounded in non-repeatable biblical events like Paul's Macedonian call in Acts 16. This left the young people looking for some vision-like message from God to call them into ministry and missions. Perhaps as bad were the times when people would bury "the call" deep in a fog bank with statements like, "I can't tell you what it is, but you will know it when you have it." Now God's call has been moved into the realm of mystical experience—something that is not explainable but definitely felt. And then you would occasionally hear someone make a statement like, "I really would like to do something else, but God has called me to do this."

---

[115] C. E. B. Cranfield, *Romans: A Shorter Commentary* (Grand Rapids: Eerdmans, 1985), 262.

[116] Timothy C. Wallstrom, *The Creation of a Student Volunteer Movement to Evangelize the World* (Pasadena, CA: William Carey International University Press, 1980), 20-22.

The net result of these mixed messages was a deep sense of confusion for many young people. Their conclusions, based on this kind of thinking, were that God would either send a message to them, or somehow make them know they were called, or that God would make them do what they didn't want to do. As one very interested in seeing young people commit to the Lord's work at home and around the world, I was intensely bothered by the muddled way in which we spoke and taught God's people about His call to service. Yet, I could not bring myself to embrace fully the alternative position, being promoted by books like *Decision Making and the Will of God*,[117] that God is not doing any special work to direct pastors and missionaries into their life's work.

## *The Characteristics of God's Call*

The great problem I experienced as a youth pastor was the lack of biblical clarity about what the call of God to ministry or missions was like. While it is impossible to eliminate subjectivity from an issue like this, we need to guard ourselves against a total surrender to subjectivity and experientialism. God's work in the life of a believer will always contain an element of mystery, but that is something very different from endorsing mysticism. Through examining the Scriptures, we can build a solid biblical framework for evaluating God's call on our lives. The rest of the chapter will explain four biblical principles about the call to ministry:

- God's call is grounded in a biblical command, not feelings.
- God's call is governed by godly dedication, not human ambition.
- God's call is given through a settled conviction, not special communication.
- God's call is confirmed by the believing community, not personal autonomy.

---

[117] Garry Friessen, *Decision Making and the Will of God* (Portland, OR: Multnomah, 1980).

## God's Call is Grounded in a Biblical Command, Not Feelings

Contrary to many people's view of missions, the primary motivation for missions should not be our feelings of compassion for human needs. Compassion is a vital part of effective ministry and should stir our hearts into ministry, but we must build from a stronger foundation than feelings. God's people have been given a responsibility and have been commanded to carry out the Great Commission. Conviction to obey God's commands forms the bedrock of God's call because it exalts God to first place in our lives. We live for Him and demonstrate our love for Him through obedience (John 14:15).

In 2 Corinthians 5:17-20, Paul sets forth the case that those who have been reconciled *to* God have received *from* God a ministry of reconciliation. Notice carefully the argument that he makes in these verses:

> Therefore if anyone is in Christ, he is a new creature; the old things passed away; behold, new things have come. Now all these things are from God, who reconciled us to Himself through Christ and gave us the ministry of reconciliation, namely, that God was in Christ reconciling the world to Himself, not counting their trespasses against them, and He has committed to us the word of reconciliation. Therefore, we are ambassadors for Christ, as though God were making an appeal through us; we beg you on behalf of Christ, be reconciled to God.

Some might be inclined to see "the ministry of reconciliation" (v. 18) as given only to the apostles, but the context seems to indicate differently.[118] Verse 18 presents the scope of the reconciliation provided ("who reconciled us to Himself") as parallel to those who have received the ministry of reconciliation ("gave us the ministry of reconciliation"). The verse preceding (v. 17) indicates that this ministry grows out of being new creations in Christ, and that is true

---

[118] For a view contrary to mine, see Paul Barnett, *The Second Epistle to the Corinthians*, NICNT (Grand Rapids: Eerdmans, 1997), 304-305.

126

of "anyone [who] is in Christ." Finally, Paul has already expanded the discussion of his own ministry to include all believers. Verses 10 and 11 speak of the judgment seat of Christ to which all believers must give account. It is based on that accountability that he persuades men, words that clearly are developed further in the following verses. The kind of persuasion to which Paul is referring is clearly stated in verse 20, "Therefore, we are ambassadors for Christ, as though God were making an appeal through us; we beg you on behalf of Christ, be reconciled to God."

The command to take the gospel to the ends of the earth is not a job reserved for specialists, it is the obligation of the entire body of believers. We all must participate in the Great Commission! The real issue which confronts every believer is not whether they need to do it, but *what will they do* to fulfill the Great Commission. Disinterest in missions is disobedience! We are commanded at the very least to pray for (Matt. 9:36-38), provide for (3 John 5-8), and participate in the sending of missionaries (Acts 13:1-4). Failure to obey God in these areas destroys the foundation upon which a call to missions is built. And anyone called to missions must base their resolve on these commands, not on fleeting emotions or on their own inconsistent ability to be compassionate.

## God's Call Is Governed by Godly Dedication, Not Human Ambition

The United States Navy may appeal to recruits with the call to adventure and the Marines may appeal with the ambition of becoming a mighty warrior, but God recruits servants as cross-bearers, not ambition-seekers. Missionaries go out to make God's name known, not to make a name for themselves. It is essential, then, that we focus on being godly people, not on recruiting numbers. God works *in* a life before He works *through* that life. What kind of godly dedication marks the life that God will direct into missions? A person God will use in missions will embrace God's purpose, commit to God's perspective, operate by God's priorities, and reflect God's purity.

A person dedicated to God will embrace God's purpose for all things—His own glory. Since God's glory is the goal and driving force of missions, those who engage in missions must be committed to that truth above all others. This is precisely why Paul expressed his driving focus in life so clearly in 2 Corinthians 5:9, "Therefore we also have as our ambition, whether at home or absent, to be pleasing to Him." If our highest ambition is to be pleasing to Him, then we will seek what He seeks—His glory (cf. 1 Cor. 10:31; Eph. 3:21). And we will aim to please Him even if it means others will not be pleased (cf. Gal. 1:10; 1 Thess. 2:4). It even means that we, like Paul, will be prepared to accept His sovereign control and endure whatever costs are needed to carry out His will and enjoy His power on our lives.

Paul provides a powerfully clear demonstration of embracing God's purpose in 2 Corinthians 12:7-10:

> Because of the surpassing greatness of the revelations, for this reason, to keep me from exalting myself, there was given me a thorn in the flesh, a messenger of Satan to torment me—to keep me from exalting myself! Concerning this I implored the Lord three times that it might leave me. And He has said to me, "My grace is sufficient for you, for power is perfected in weakness." Most gladly, therefore, I will rather boast about my weaknesses, so that the power of Christ may dwell in me. Therefore I am well content with weaknesses, with insults, with distresses, with persecutions, with difficulties, for Christ's sake; for when I am weak, then I am strong.

For Paul, if God's glory needed to be displayed through these afflictions, then he "most gladly" would boast in them and be content with them. He knew that the "treasure" was "in earthen vessels, so that the surpassing greatness of the power will be of God and not from ourselves" (2 Cor. 4:7). Because he embraced God's ultimate purpose, he was able to embrace God's immediate purposes, even if that meant suffering for him. That kind of life is fertile territory for a missionary call!

Second, they will be committed to God's perspective on all things. The life that God will use for His service is a life of faith. 2 Corinthians 5:7 sets forth a basic principle of Christian living, "we walk by faith, not by sight." What that statement means has already been made clear by 4:16-18:

> Therefore we do not lose heart, but though our outer man is decaying, yet our inner man is being renewed day by day. For momentary, light affliction is producing for us an eternal weight of glory far beyond all comparison, while we look not at the things which are seen, but at the things which are not seen; for the things which are seen are temporal, but the things which are not seen are eternal.

Being committed to God's perspective on all things means we see things by faith in the light of eternity and by the light of the Scriptures, the basis and content of our faith. God gave us His Word as an infallible guide for life that reveals His will and tells us how He views things. Spiritual maturity is looking at life from God's perspective as revealed in the Word. Seeing the purpose of life from an eternal viewpoint changes the way we go about living. Seeing the problems of life from a God-centered viewpoint changes the way we respond to them. Seeing the path of life from God's perspective changes the way we make choices.

Third, they will operate by God's priorities in all things. If we are seeing things from God's perspective, it will change our value system and be reflected in our life priorities. As 2 Corinthians 4:16-18 demonstrated, we will not live for things that are temporal. Our lives will be controlled by things that are eternal, that matter when this life is over. In contrast, a life consumed with the pursuit of this world's pleasures and treasures will be deaf to the call of God to leave them in order to take the gospel to some far corner of the world. Even some good priorities like family can become imbalanced to the point where we make them more important than God and His global purpose to call out a people for His name.

Fourth, they will reflect God's purity in all things. With the kind of boldness that could cause us to blush, Paul clearly articulated his concern for personal purity in his life and ministry:

> For our proud confidence is this: the testimony of our conscience, that in holiness and godly sincerity, not in fleshly wisdom but in the grace of God, we have conducted ourselves in the world, and especially toward you (2 Cor. 1:12).

Since Paul set his focus continually on God, his great concern in life and ministry was to reflect God's holy character. And he recognized that the great promise of close fellowship with God required separation from sin. After exhorting the Corinthians to break off any relationships that contradicted their character as God's people and temple, he calls on them to "cleanse [them]selves from all defilement of flesh and spirit, perfecting holiness in the fear of God" (2 Cor. 7:1). A conscience continually defiled by sin is not going to be sensitive to the call of God into ministry and missions. We cannot continually *ignore* God about sin and expect to *hear* Him about service.

## God's Call is Given through a Settled Conviction, not Special Communication

Although the "call" is frequently described in terms that sound like speech, most conservative Christians do not really mean that we hear God's voice audibly or by means of a dream or vision. In that sense, we should use passages like Acts 13:1-4 and 16:9-10 very carefully. These accounts offer valuable truth about the principle of God's calling (*that* He does it), but should not be taken as providing a pattern for God's calling (*how* He does it).[119] Clearly the Macedonian call (16:9-10) was special revelation from God and should not be viewed as the normal pattern for believers today, and the call of Saul and Barnabas (13:1-4) was probably mediated through revelation given by the Spirit to one of the prophets mentioned in verse one.[120] Of course, we can add to these two historical references the conversion and call of the Apostle Paul recorded in Acts 9, and to which he regularly referred (e.g., Rom. 1:1, 1 Cor. 1:1, Gal. 1:1, 15). Yet most would concede again that

---

[119] I recognize that some are not even comfortable with this view, that is, they believe that the presence of special revelation in these cases makes them inapplicable to believers after such revelation has ceased.

[120] Cf., I. Howard Marshall, *Acts* (Grand Rapids: Eerdmans, 1980), 216.

Paul's call does not serve as a pattern for ours. But there is clear evidence that God works specifically to direct servants into ministry and missions. We will examine a number of texts related to ministry and missions to help us see how God supplies leaders for His work, sends leaders into the work, and stirs leaders to do the work.

### God Supplies the Leaders for the Work

Acts 20 records a meeting between the Apostle Paul and the elders of the church in Ephesus, and verse 28 provides insight into how these men became leaders in God's work: "Be on guard for yourselves and for all the flock, *among which the Holy Spirit has made you overseers*, to shepherd the church of God which He purchased with His own blood."

Paul indicates that the Holy Spirit is instrumental in setting men apart for the work of the ministry. The text does not indicate specifically how the Spirit made them such, but the implication is that they "were manifestly men on whom the Holy Spirit had bestowed the requisite qualifications for the work."[121] Marshall goes so far as to say, "Such people owed their appointment to God's choice of them by the Spirit."[122] As we will see later, God's choice is mediated in connection with God's people, but to remove God from active involvement in the process is to ignore the force of this text.

This truth is also established in Ephesians 4:11-12, "And He gave some as apostles, and some as prophets, and some as evangelists, and some as pastors and teachers, for the equipping of the saints for the work of service, to the building up of the body of Christ." We know from the verses that precede it, that the "He" of verse 11 is the risen Lord, Jesus Christ. The text says that the risen Christ "gave" men to the church to serve in ministry capacities that would equip the church so that it could reach its God-intended goal. O'Brien's comments on this text bring clearly into focus its importance to the issue we are examining:

---

[121] F. F. Bruce, *The Book of Acts*, NICNT (Grand Rapids: Eerdmans, 1954), 416.

[122] Marshall, *Acts*, 333.

While in 1 Corinthians 12:4-11 the "varieties of gifts" are diverse ministries allocated by the Spirit and the ability to exercise them, here the gifts are the persons themselves, "given" by the ascended Christ to his people to enable them to function and develop as they should. Christ supplies the church with gifted ministers.[123]

As with Acts 20:28, the text does not tell us how the Lord does this, but that is no grounds for ignoring the fact that He clearly is active in providing gifted men for His work.

Of particular importance to the cause of missions is the group identified as "evangelists." Though our common terminology makes a distinction between evangelists and missionaries, it is best to see missionary work as included in this term.[124] Some see a close connection between the roles of apostle and evangelist. Bruce states that the "evangelists given by the ascended Christ continued to exercise the gospel-preaching aspect of the apostolic ministry, so that the church might grow in succeeding generations by the adhesion of new believers."[125] Peters takes it a step further:

> A careful study leads to the conclusion that a New Testament evangelist is an apostle, fully responsible for the apostolic function minus the apostolic office and original authority. Thus the evangelist continues the function of being the *sent one* for the same purpose the apostles were sent—to preach the gospel, preach the Word, evangelize communities and establish churches—but he does not possess the original apostolic office, authority and rank.[126]

---

[123] Peter T. O'Brien, *The Letter to the Ephesians* (Grand Rapids: Eerdmans, 1999), 297.

[124] Homer A. Kent, Jr., *Ephesians: The Glory of the Church* (Chicago: Moody, 1971), p 71.

[125] F. F. Bruce, *The Epistles to the Colossians, to Philemon, and to the Ephesians,* NICNT (Grand Rapids: Eerdmans, 1984), 347.

[126] George W. Peters, *A Biblical Theology of Missions* (Chicago: Moody, 1972), 247.

Given the limited biblical material about the office of evangelist, it is difficult to justify the kind of dogmatism that Peters displays.[127] But it is clear that Philip, the only one called an evangelist in the New Testament (Acts 21:8), did do the work of taking the gospel to new places and peoples—the Samaritans, the Ethiopian eunuch, and to all the cities between Azotus and Caesarea (Acts 8). Regardless of the precise definition of the function of an evangelist, it is clear that such a role is a gift from Christ to His body. Christ has provided evangelists to expand the church by proclaiming Him among people who have not heard.

This principle is also reflected in Paul's words to Archippus through the letter to the Colossians, "Take heed to the ministry which you have received in the Lord, that you may fulfill it" (4:17). The basis for this exhortation is that "the ministry" that Archippus was to fulfill was to be viewed as something given to him by the Lord.[128] The thought is similar to that of Ephesians 4:11, that is, "all Christian service…was both gift (Rom. 12:7; 1 Cor. 12:5) and commission from the Lord Christ."[129] Harris goes so far as to suggest one way of understanding the phrase "received in the Lord" is "at the Lord's bidding."[130] As we have seen in the other texts, it is the Lord who is actively supplying workers for His church.

### God Sends the Leaders into the Work

God not only selects leaders *for* the church; He also sends them *out of* the church, into the harvest to proclaim the gospel. In Matthew 9:37-38, Jesus instructs His disciples, "The harvest is plentiful, but the workers are few. Therefore beseech the Lord of the harvest to send out workers into His harvest." Since this text commands us to pray for God to send laborers into the harvest, God must actually do

---

[127] Perhaps it is necessary to say that no precise identification can be espoused too dogmatically for the very same reason. The term itself leaves latitude as to the place where the function of evangelist can be exercised.

[128] Richard R. Melick, Jr., *Philippians, Colossians, Philemon* (Nashville: Broadman, 1991), 332.

[129] James D. G. Dunn, *The Epistles to the Colossians and to Philemon* (Grand Rapids: Eerdmans, 1996), 288.

[130] Murray J. Harris, *Colossians & Philemon* (Grand Rapids: Eerdmans, 1991), 214.

just that. In other words, if God does not actually direct people into missions, then why does Jesus command us to pray for Him to do it?

We have already seen this language of sending in Romans 10:15a, "How will they preach unless they are sent?" The One who sends is God Himself and, in that sense, this text fits well with Matthew 9:37-38. Just as Christ told us to pray for the Father to send laborers, Paul tells us that these laborers must be sent in order to see the harvest brought in. The implication of both texts is that God is sovereign over the harvest and active in the process of sending laborers into it. John Broadus sets the proper balance into clear perspective:

> Such laborers as the Lord of the harvest does put forth, we may endeavor, with his blessing, to train for the better performance of their work; but they must be his laborers, not ours, called into the work, and urged to the performance of it, by himself.[131]

### God Stirs Leaders to Do the Work

So how then does God give the call to ministry or missions? If we rule out special revelation, must we rule out the work of God in definitively directing a person into missions? Is the pursuit of missionary service only a vocational choice or career decision? Such responses move too far in the other direction and do not pay sufficient heed to what God has said He will do in His people to accomplish His purposes.

For example, one of the great motivations of the Christian life is the truth that "it is God who is at work in you, both to will and to work for His good pleasure" (Phil. 2:13). This text instructs us that God's work in our lives produces both *desire* and *action* ("to will and to work"). The transforming grace of God will affect the internal desires of a believer directing him toward His good pleasure, that which is pleasing to Him. Consider Hebrews 13:20-21:

> Now the God of peace, who brought up from the dead the great Shepherd of the sheep through the blood of the eternal

---

[131] John Broadus, *Matthew* (Valley Forge: Judson Press, 1886), 212.

covenant, even Jesus our Lord, equip you in every good thing to do His will, working in us that which is pleasing in His sight, through Jesus Christ, to whom be the glory forever and ever. Amen.

Here, as in Philippians 2:13, it is God who works, and His work focuses on equipping believers with all that they need to do His will, enabling them to be "pleasing in His sight."

God's saving work encompasses more than changing the eternal destination of the one who is saved. In the words of Ephesians 2:10, believers "are His workmanship, created in Christ Jesus for good works, which God prepared beforehand so that we would walk in them." God equips believers to do His will by energizing them to will and work for what pleases Him. It seems reasonable to conclude, based simply on these principles, that a believer's service for Christ is a vital part of God's work in the life of that believer. Service is the outgrowth of God's inner working. Although drawn from the Old Testament, Nehemiah serves as a good example of how these principles would operate. His testimony indicates this kind of direction from God, "I did not tell anyone what my God was putting into my mind to do for Jerusalem" (Neh. 2:12). Here God works within the believer to direct his mind (lit. heart) toward the work that God wanted done for His cause.

The same work happens in the lives of those called to pastoral ministry. 1 Timothy 3:1 begins the discussion of qualification for ministry with the words, "if any man aspires to the office of overseer, it is a fine work he desires to do." This crucial passage on pastoral ministry says nothing directly about a call, but what it says about aspiring and desiring the office is, based on the discussion above, the equivalent of it. God places a desire for ministry into the heart of a man as the means of directing him into the work. Charles Bridges' classic on ministry rightly identifies the important role of desire as an evidence of God's work in calling a man to ministry:

> The Apostle strongly marks *a constraining desire* as a primary Ministerial qualification; something far beyond the general Christian desire to promote the glory of God—a special

kindling within—in character, if not intensity, like "the burning fire shut up" in the prophet's bosom, and overcoming his determination to go back from the service of his God. This constraint rises above all difficulties, takes pleasure in sacrifices for the work's sake, and quickens to a readiness of mind...[132]

Of course, desire alone is not enough to admit a man to the office of overseer, as is clear from the list of qualifications that follow in verses 2-7. As Bridges wrote almost two centuries ago: "The desire, (though correctly answering to the standard of intensity, consideration, and purity) does not of itself attest a Divine vocation. We cannot suppose the Lord to send unqualified laborers, *however willing*, into his vineyard: and none but he can qualify them."[133]

Sadly, it is too common to hear people talk about the ministry or missions as if it were the last thing on earth that they want to do, but they somehow feel they have to do it. God expects just the opposite attitude from those who serve in ministry—they do it not because they have to, but because God has placed in them a consuming desire to do so. Peter addressed this attitude quite clearly when he exhorted the elders to "shepherd the flock of God among you, exercising oversight *not under compulsion, but voluntarily*, according to the will of God; and not for sordid gain, but with eagerness" (1 Pet. 5:2). Ministerial labor is to be done with a spirit of voluntary surrender that eagerly pursues God's will. The picture of pastors and missionaries being dragged kicking and screaming into their place of service is contrary to the Scriptures and the work of God.

Make no mistake about it, a man will feel compelled to do the work of God, but this compulsion is something that God has *worked into* the man, not *forced upon* him from outside. God will be at work in him to "will and work for His good pleasure" and God's call will become clear through the deep sense of purpose placed in the heart by God. In other words, the pursuit of ministry and missions should be based

---

[132] Charles Bridges, *The Christian Ministry*, reprint (Carlisle, PA: Banner of Truth, 1959), pp. 94-95.
[133] Ibid., p. 99.

on something more than the feeling that "I could do this." It should be empowered by the deep, settled conviction that this is what God wants me to do in order to carry out His good pleasure.

## God's Call Is Confirmed by the Believing Community, Not Personal Autonomy

The last characteristic of God's call is that it is to be confirmed by the believing community. Sometimes people suggest that the thing that really matters is following God's call whether anyone else recognizes it or not. However, this is out of step with the pattern of Scripture, where individuals were set apart for the ministry by the local church, not apart from it. God directed Saul and Barnabas into the work of missions within the context of the local church and through the ministry of the local church (cf. Acts 13:1-4). Schools, mission boards, and non-profits do not send out missionaries; local churches do.

The question of giftedness for the task of ministry and missions must be asked and answered within the context of local church ministry. The gifts were given for ministry *within* the church (1 Cor. 12:28, "God has appointed in the church") and *for* the church (1 Cor. 12:7, "But to each one is given the manifestation of the Spirit for the common good"). Ordination is the process of recognition by the church of the gifts given by God to the candidate for ministry (1 Tim. 4:14; 2 Tim. 1:6). If a man is not "able to teach" (1 Tim. 3:2) and not able to hold "fast the faithful word which is in accordance with the teaching, so that he will be able both to exhort in sound doctrine and to refute those who contradict" (Titus 1:9), then that man is not qualified for leadership in the local church, whether at home or on the foreign field. And these gifts cannot be displayed or evaluated apart from the community of believers. It is there that the ministry of the Word centers and from there that the ministers of the Word are chosen and sent.

The other qualifications for ministry listed in 1 Timothy 3:2-7, Titus 1:6-9, and 1 Peter 5:2-3 must be examined in the context of the local church. If he does not have the character described in these verses, a man is not qualified for the work. And appointing an unqualified man can have dire consequences for the church. As Paul warns in 1 Timothy 5:22, "Do not lay hands upon anyone too hastily and thereby share responsibility for the sins of others; keep yourself free from sin." Setting someone apart for God's work (laying hands upon them) is to be done carefully, after having examined character, evident giftedness, and devotion to the task. Paul makes it plain to Timothy that the instructions given in the qualifications list are intended to provide divine instruction about "how one ought to conduct himself in the household of God, which is the church of the living God, the pillar and support of the truth" (1 Tim. 3:15). This passage is clearly referring to the local church since this verse follows directly on the heels of instructions about appointing overseers and deacons. A local church then, rather than the universal church, must assess whether a man is qualified for ministry.

Willingness to go to the mission field is not the sole requirement for doing so. A candidate for missionary service must be recognized by God's people as qualified for that service. Without that recognition, the question of God's call remains unanswered. We have too often neglected the role of God's people in the process of confirming God's call on an individual's life. The subjective belief of the individual himself must be confirmed by the assessment of God's people. Our American culture prides itself on personal autonomy and rugged individualism, but the pursuit of God's call is not based on these traits. When God is calling someone to ministry, He imparts a compelling desire, genuine godliness, and the appropriate gifts, and He causes His people to recognize His hand upon that person. None of these alone is evidence of God's call, but together they form a powerful witness to the work of God in sending out workers into the harvest.

*"All the inhabitants of the earth are accounted as nothing, But He does according to His will in the host of heaven And among the inhabitants of earth; And no one can ward off His hand Or say to Him, 'What have You done?'*

Daniel 4:35

# 8

# GOD'S SOVEREIGNTY AND THE SPREAD OF THE GOSPEL

*This last chapter was originally written as a journal article, and as such, has more formal tone than the rest of the book. But I felt that it would be a good reference point for those who want to dive more deeply into the theological motivations for missions. The chapters that have gone before established that God's glory in salvation is the ultimate goal of missions. God's sovereign control over all things including the spread of the gospel through individual conversions gives us reason to give all the glory to Him alone. This chapter will examine how the doctrines of divine sovereignty not only do not dampen missions activity, but actually empower it.*

The relationship between God's sovereignty and the tasks of evangelism and missions is often a central point of tension. There is ample evidence from church history that belief in God's sovereign control, even in salvation, provided the kindling for the Great Awakening and the modern missionary movement,[134] but people often object that believing in God's sovereignty leads to unbiblical positions on evangelism and missions such as:

• Believing that God is sovereign in salvation makes evangelism and missions unnecessary—if the elect will all be saved, then we don't need to worry about telling them or sending missionaries to them.

---

[134] E.g., Timothy George's biography of William Carey, *Faithful Witness: The Life and Mission of William Carey* (Birmingham, AL: New Hope, 1991), 47–66.

- Believing that God is sovereign in salvation makes evangelism and missions illegitimate and unethical—how can you tell a group of people that God will save them when it is possible that they are non-elect?

Obviously, these objections, if true, are serious errors. The second one focuses on the free offer of the gospel and is not the direct focus of this article. The focus in this article will be on the first objection— does belief in God's sovereign bestowal of the gift of salvation deaden the evangelistic and missionary impulse?

Before we tackle this question, it might be appropriate to lay down a caution about this whole approach to the discussion: is a mistake to make evangelistic zeal or missionary motivation the test of biblical truth. In principle, our first commitment must be to "accurately handling the word of truth" Only after we find out what the Scriptures actually say can we think through the ramifications of that truth. It is difficult to focus on exegesis before application (perhaps impossible to do completely), but it is the goal toward which we ought to strive. In other words, the approach should be to ask, "What does the Bible teach about salvation?" before we ask, "How does this relate to our commission to proclaim the gospel and engage in missions?" And the answers to both of these questions must be derived from the Scriptures!

In any event, the question to be considered is, "Does believing in God's sovereignty deaden evangelistic zeal and missionary motivation?" Before this question can be answered, it will be necessary to define more precisely what is meant by God's sovereignty. Most believers agree that God is sovereign, but their understanding of that truth is often radically divergent. So this chapter will first define a biblical position on divine sovereignty. Following this definition, I will approach the primary question from two angles—defensive and offensive. In other words, I want to defend belief in sovereign grace against this accusation and then set forth a case for how these doctrines actually provide positive incentive for both evangelism and missions.

## *God is Sovereign Over All Things, Including Salvation*

Although most believers agree that God is sovereign, there is considerably less agreement about what that means. Additionally, not all views of God's sovereignty are charged with the criticism of being detrimental to evangelism and missions. Some take God's sovereignty to mean simply that He rules over all things, but not that He has planned or controls all things. Bruce Reichenbach embraces such a view of sovereignty:

> God is a sovereign, not a novelist. He does not purpose or dispose everything that happens; his purposes are both general and specific, but they do not include every detail of human existence. Not only does he work through his created natural law, but just as importantly he has (in part) entrusted his program to the hands and feet of people. This means, of course, that at times his plans and purposes are thwarted.[135]

There are two assertions here that need to be addressed: 1) that God's purpose or plan does not include everything that happens; and 2) that God's purposes may at times be thwarted. Both of these represent a novel approach to God's sovereignty that departs from the one presented in the Scriptures. Logically, it seems that the question of whether God's purposes can be thwarted takes precedence over whether He has a purpose for all things, so the assertions will be considered in that order.

Claiming that God's purposes may be thwarted allows maximum latitude for man's freedom, but it contradicts the conclusion Job reached when confronted with God's sovereignty. His assessment was, "I know that You can do all things, and that no purpose of Yours can be thwarted" (Job 42:2). In fact, the ability to carry out all that He has planned is what distinguishes the true and living God from all pretender gods. Consider God's own claim, "Remember

---

[135] "God Limits His Power," in *Predestination and Free Will: Four Views of Divine Sovereignty and Human Freedom*, ed. David Basinger and Randall Basinger (Wheaton, IL: InterVarsity, 1986), 117.

the former things long past, for I am God, and there is no other; I am God, and there is no one like Me, declaring the end from the beginning, and from ancient times things which have not been done, saying, 'My purpose will be established, and I will accomplish all My good pleasure'" (Isa. 46:9–10). Contrary to the claims of those who trim the concept of God's sovereignty in order to argue for a larger view of man's freedom, the Bible leaves no room for the purposes of God to go unfulfilled or be left unaccomplished.

If people concede that none of God's purposes can be thwarted, then their efforts to argue for a general kind of sovereignty tend to follow the line of Reichenbach's first assertion, namely, that God does not have a purpose for all things. Boyd recognizes this: "To confess that God can control whatever he wants to control leaves open the question of *how much* God actually does want to control."[136] The crucial question, then, is whether God has a plan which encompasses all things.

## *God is Sovereign Over All Things*

Ephesians 1:11 plainly states that God "works all things after the counsel of His will." This is a profound declaration of the fact that "whatever [God] has planned and decided to do will certainly come to pass."[137] God's sovereign freedom is a point of praise in the Psalms: "But our God is in the heavens; He does whatever He pleases" (115:3); "Whatever the Lord pleases, He does, in heaven and in earth, in the seas and in all deeps" (135:6). The biblical evidence reveals that all the events of life are under God's sovereign control:

- Birth and death—The Lord kills and makes alive; He brings down to Sheol and raises up (1 Sam. 2:6).
- The rise and fall of rulers—Every person is to be in subjection to the governing authorities. For there is no authority except from God, and those which exist are

---

[136] Greg Boyd, *The God of the Possible* (Grand Rapids: Baker, 2000), 51.

[137] Peter T. O'Brien, *The Letter to the Ephesians*, PNTC (Grand Rapids: Eerdmans, 1999), 117.

established by God (Rom. 13:1); But God is the Judge; He puts down one and exalts another (Ps. 75:7).

- The direction a king pursues is in His hand—The king's heart is like channels of water in the hand of the Lord; He turns it wherever He wishes (Prov. 21:1).
- Both bounty and calamity come from His hand—Is it not from the mouth of the Most High that both good and ill go forth? (Lam. 3:38); In the day of prosperity be happy, but in the day of adversity consider—God has made the one as well as the other so that man will not discover anything that will be after him (Eccl. 7:14).
- Even the casting of a lot comes under God's control—The lot is cast into the lap, but its every decision is from the Lord (Prov. 16:33).

The Scriptures also teach that even the sinful acts of the devil and men are under His control and serve His purposes. The biblical record regarding Satan's attacks against Job proves this. Satan had to have permission from God: "Then the Lord said to Satan, 'Behold, all that he has is in your power, only do not put forth your hand on him.' So Satan departed from the presence of the Lord" (Job 1:12); "So the Lord said to Satan, 'Behold, he is in your power, only spare his life'" (Job 2:6). Job, confronted by the calamities in chapter 1, responds, confirming God's sovereign control: "Then Job arose and tore his robe and shaved his head, and he fell to the ground and worshiped. He said, 'Naked I came from my mother's womb, and naked I shall return there. The Lord gave and the Lord has taken away. Blessed be the name of the Lord'" (vv. 20-21).

Clearly Job recognized that these events could not have happened apart from the sovereign control of God. And if Job's conclusion is not sufficient proof, consider the words of the Lord Himself to Satan regarding Job, "he still holds fast his integrity, although you incited Me against him to ruin him without cause" (Job 2:3b).[138] There is no room in that text for escaping the conclusion that Satan's attacks on Job were very much under God's sovereign control.

---

[138] I am grateful to Dr. Robert Bell for bringing this text to my attention.

The biblical account of Joseph also confirms this exhaustive view of God's sovereign control. Consider Joseph's response to his brothers in Genesis 50:20: "As for you, you meant evil against me, but God meant it for good in order to bring about this present result, to preserve many people alive." D. A. Carson effectively draws out the ramifications of Joseph's statement:

> He does not picture the event as wicked human machination into which God intervened to bring forth good. Nor does he imagine God's intention had been to send him down there with a fine escort and a modern chariot but that unfortunately the brothers mucked up the plan, and so poor old Joseph had to go down there as a slave—sorry about that. Rather, in one and the same event, God was operating, and his intentions were good, and the brothers were operating, and their intentions were evil.[139]

The crucifixion of Jesus Christ likewise demonstrates that even the sinful acts of men fall within the eternal plan of God. Peter makes this point clearly in his sermon on Pentecost: "This Man, delivered over by the predetermined plan and foreknowledge of God, you nailed to a cross by the hands of godless men and put Him to death" (Acts 2:23). And Peter was not alone in this belief. Believers prayed in Acts 4:27–28: "For truly in this city there were gathered together against Your holy servant Jesus, whom You anointed, both Herod and Pontius Pilate, along with the Gentiles and the peoples of Israel, to do whatever Your hand and Your purpose predestined to occur." God's plan, established long before, included these sinful actions (without ever violating God's holiness).

The point of tension focuses on how God's sovereignty relates to human responsibility. Historically, both Calvinists and Arminians have agreed that God does indeed have an eternal plan which controls all things.[140] Their point of disagreement focused on the

---

[139] D. A. Carson, *The Difficult Doctrine of the Love of God* (Wheaton, IL: Crossway, 2000), 52.

[140] Robert E. Picirilli, *Grace, Faith, Free Will* (Nashville, TN: Randall House, 2002), 35, 44.

relationship of God's foreknowledge to His eternal plan. The Arminian position argued that God's knowledge of what men would do was the basis for the determination of His will. It is important to recognize, however, that both of these historic positions view present choices as certain because of God's eternal plan.[141] Returning to the Acts texts, to acknowledge that God's plan encompasses even the sinful acts of humans is, then, something common to all historic, orthodox Christianity, not merely the Calvinistic understanding of it.[142]

God's sovereignty over all things, including an all-inclusive plan which makes all future events certain, has been the historic belief of God's people. The major views have attempted to simultaneously maintain the biblical teaching about God's sovereignty and human responsibility. Although each view believes that the other fails to do so adequately, neither has openly denied either God's sovereignty or human responsibility.

## God is Sovereign Over Personal Salvation

At no place is the tension between the various views of God's sovereignty been highlighted more clearly than regarding the matter of personal salvation. Again, all orthodox believers would assent to God's sovereignty in this area, but their respective understandings of it would be considerably different. At the risk of oversimplification, the dividing line seems to focus on the biblical concept of election. Wayne Grudem's definition of election is helpful for narrowing the discussion and tying it to the subject of this chapter: "Election is an act of God before creation in which he

---

[141] Ibid., p. 36. Greg Boyd acknowledges this agreement and argues that both, therefore, result in a "future that is eternally settled and that God eternally knows it as such." Against this, Boyd argues for an open future (*The God of the Possible*, 23).

[142] For persuasive arguments that Open Theism represents a departure from historic, orthodox Christianity, see Bruce A. Ware, *God's Lesser Glory* (Wheaton, IL: Crossway, 2000) or John M. Frame, *No Other God* (Phillipsburg, NJ: P & R, 2001).

chooses some people to be saved, not on account of any foreseen merit in them, but only because of his sovereign good pleasure."[143]

Not all who embrace God's sovereignty over personal salvation would be willing to embrace this definition of election. And, generally speaking, it would be those who reject this understanding of election that make the charge that such a belief is detrimental to evangelism and missions. A full defense of this view is beyond the scope of this chapter, but a brief examination of the teachings of Jesus Christ found in John 6 will serve to bring the issues more clearly into focus.

## God's Sovereignty in Giving Some to the Son

Jesus taught that there was a group of people who were given to Him by the Father, and these are the ones who will come to Him: "All that the Father gives Me will come to Me, and the one who comes to Me I will certainly not cast out" (v. 37). Note the argument that the Lord makes here: those given to Him by the Father are the ones that come to Him. What does He mean by the words, "All that the Father gives Me"? The other uses of this language in John's gospel shed light on its meaning:

- This is the will of Him who sent Me, that of all that He has given Me I lose nothing, but raise it up on the last day (John 6:39).
- My Father, who has given them to Me, is greater than all; and no one is able to snatch them out of the Father's hand (John 10:29).
- Even as You gave Him authority over all flesh, that to all whom You have given Him, He may give eternal life (John 17:2).
- I have manifested Your name to the men whom You gave Me out of the world; they were Yours and You gave them to Me, and they have kept Your word (John 17:6).
- I ask on their behalf; I do not ask on behalf of the world, but of those whom You have given Me; for they are Yours (John 17:9).

---

[143] *Systematic Theology* (Grand Rapids: Zondervan, 1994), 670.

- Father, I desire that they also, whom You have given Me, be with Me where I am, so that they may see My glory which You have given Me, for You loved Me before the foundation of the world (John 17:24).
- To fulfill the word which He spoke, "Of those whom You have given Me I lost not one" (John 18:9).

John 17:2 seems to be particularly clear in establishing this point and brings this issue into penetrating focus—the Son has authority over all flesh, but He will give life only to those whom the Father has given to Him. The language is clear that the purpose of Christ's receiving authority is to give life to those who were given to Him. Laney captures it well:

> The purpose clause, introduced by "that" (*hina*), reveals the purpose for which Christ received His authority. The divine authority possessed by Jesus was for the specific purpose of conferring "eternal life" (3:15–16; 3:35–36; 5:24; 10:28). Yet this gift is not conferred indiscriminately. It is granted only to the elect—those "given" to Christ by the Father (cf. 6:37).[144]

This same truth is taught in 5:21 ("For just as the Father raises the dead and gives them life, even so the Son also gives life to whom He wishes") and 17:9 ("I ask on their behalf; I do not ask on behalf of the world, but of those whom You have given Me; for they are Yours"). These texts affirm that God's will regarding eternal life is both determinative ("to whom He wishes") and discriminating ("not...on behalf of the world, but of those whom You have given Me").

Contrary to our contemporary hesitancy about these truths, the Lord confronted those who rejected Him with them. Consider His powerful words to another group of rejecters:

> But you do not believe because you are not of My sheep. My sheep hear My voice, and I know them, and they follow Me;

---

[144] J. Carl Laney, *John* (Chicago: Moody Press, 1992), 301.

and I give eternal life to them, and they will never perish; and no one will snatch them out of My hand. My Father, who has given them to Me, is greater than all; and no one is able to snatch them out of the Father's hand. I and the Father are one (John 10:26–30).

Here Jesus roots their rejection ("you do not believe") in the fact that they were not His sheep. His sheep, on the contrary, "hear" His voice and "follow" Him because they were "given to" Him by the Father.

## God's Sovereignty in Drawing Them to the Son

Jesus taught that man has no ability to come to Him apart from the drawing work of the Father: "No one can come to Me unless the Father who sent Me draws him; and I will raise him up on the last day" (John 6:44). The Lord restates this truth in verse 65: "For this reason I have said to you, that no one can come to Me unless it has been granted him from the Father." Before anyone can come to Christ, there must be a preceding work by the Father to provide the ability to do so. "The responsibility of men and women in the matter of coming to Christ is not overlooked (cf. John 5:40); but none at all would come unless divinely persuaded and enabled to do so."[145]

Man's inability to respond to the gospel apart from God's gracious work is continually at the center of the debate about God's sovereignty and seems to serve as the ultimate dividing line in this debate—at some point the discussion turns to the "freedom of the will." Yet this debate often ignores the fact that both Arminian and Calvinist theologians agree that man's unaided will is in bondage to sin and unable to come to Christ.[146] The Arminian sees this inability overcome via prevenient grace, whereas the Calvinist sees it overcome via efficacious grace, but both acknowledge the inability of man apart from God's grace. Wiley, an Arminian theologian, explains this concept as follows:

---

[145] F. F. Bruce, *The Gospel of John* (Grand Rapids: Eerdmans, 1983), 156.
[146] Picirilli, *Grace, Faith, Free Will*, 151.

> Prevenient grace, as the term implies, is that grace which "goes before" or prepares the soul for entrance into the initial state of salvation. It is the preparatory grace of the Holy Spirit exercised toward man helpless in sin. As it respects the guilty, it may be considered mercy; as it respects the impotent, it is enabling power. It may be defined, therefore, as that manifestation of the divine influence which precedes the full regenerate life.[147]

It is clear from this explanation that unsaved man, even from the Arminian perspective, is both "helpless" and "impotent," and, subsequently, needs "enabling power." Picirilli acknowledges that prevenient grace, which he prefers to call "pre-regenerating grace," is necessary since "the unregenerate person is totally unable to respond positively, by his natural will, to the offer of salvation contained in the gospel."[148] And he believes that the idea of *drawing* taught in John 6:44 is an example of this pre-regenerating grace.

Prevenient grace, while absolutely necessary, may be finally resisted, so it is not to be confused with the concept of efficacious grace, that is, a grace which effectively produces a saving response to Jesus Christ. The doctrine of prevenient grace seeks to retain the right of ultimate self-determination for the sinner—he or she determines finally whether grace is to be accepted or rejected. The doctrine of efficacious grace is grounded in the belief that salvation is not ultimately determined by the will of man, but by God.

Another dimension of the prevenient grace doctrine is that such grace is extended to all who hear the gospel (versus only to some who hear the gospel).[149] But the truths that the Lord teaches in this passage run contrary to this idea. Carson demonstrates the problem for those who advocate prevenient grace from a text like John 6:44:

---

[147] H. Orton Wiley, *Christian Theology*, vol. 2 (Kansas City, MO: Beacon Hill Press, 1945), 345–46.

[148] Picirilli, *Grace, Faith, Free Will*, 154.

[149] Ibid., p. 158.

The thought of v. 44 is the negative counterpart to v. 37a. The latter tells us that all whom the Father gives to the Son will come to him; here we are told that no-one can come to him unless the Father draws him.... The combination of v. 37a and v. 44 prove that this "drawing" activity of the Father cannot be reduced to what theologians sometimes call "prevenient grace" dispensed to every individual, for this "drawing" is selective, or else the negative note in v. 44 is meaningless.[150]

It seems obvious from the passage that those to whom Jesus was speaking had actually heard the gospel; that is why Jesus is confronting their unbelief (cf. vv. 36, 64). While Picirilli correctly acknowledges that this passage teaches that God's drawing provides enabling power to come to Christ, he seems to ignore the indicators in the text that not all who heard were actually drawn by the Father to Christ.

The same truth is found in John 8:47 ("He who is of God hears the words of God; for this reason you do not hear them, because you are not of God") and 10:26–27 ("But you do not believe because you are not of My sheep. My sheep hear My voice, and I know them, and they follow Me"). In both passages the Word about Christ is being proclaimed, yet the text is clear that some can "hear" it and others cannot; the difference between them is whether one is "of God" and one of His "sheep." As Milne notes:

> Jesus' specifying the reason for the Jewish leaders' failure to believe in him as *you are not my sheep* confronts us with the mystery of divine election and human unbelief. In stressing the call of the Son and the gifting of the Father, Jesus does not eliminate the leaders' culpability for their rejection of him. Their responsibility is the unuttered premise of every word of judgment he pronounces. But behind and through their response God is also at work.[151]

---

[150] Carson, *The Gospel According to John* (Grand Rapids: Eerdmans, 1991), 293.

[151] Bruce Milne, *The Message of John*, The Bible Speaks Today, (Downers Grove, IL: InterVarsity, 1993), 154.

It seems impossible to deny that this passage teaches that no one *can* come to Christ apart from God's enabling. Attempts made to smooth the rough edge of this truth by arguing that God draws either all men [152] or, at least, all those who hear the gospel [153] fall short. The language of this passage will not allow such limitations— not all who hear the gospel are drawn by the Father, only those who have been given to the Son (vv. 37, 65).

## God's Sovereignty in Teaching Them

Another difference between the concepts of prevenient and efficacious grace is the certainty with which the latter will accomplish its purpose. Advocates of prevenient grace (God's drawing) teach that it supplies the enabling power needed to come to Christ, but it does not necessarily result in someone doing so. In the words of Picirilli, it "makes faith possible without making it necessary... it does not by itself guarantee the conversion of the sinner."[154]

This is different from the ministry of the Father described in verse 45. Here Jesus teaches that those who have "heard and learned from the Father" will indeed come to Him: "It is written in the prophets, 'and they shall all be taught of God.' Everyone who has heard and learned from the Father, comes to Me." Note the certainty of the Lord's words: "everyone" that fits a certain description "comes to Me." What is that description? Such people as have "heard and learned from the Father."

It seems clear that the words "heard and learned" are another way of referring to the drawing ministry of the Father since the result of both is coming to Christ. Kent is insightful on this point:

> The true believer, therefore, is one who hears the Word of God and that Word is interpreted to his heart by the Holy Spirit. In this way God acts upon men's hearts and creates that spiritual attraction toward Christ that draws men to

---

[152] Hunt (*What Love Is This?* 338) argues that "the Father is drawing everyone (even through the witness of creation and conscience)."

[153] Picirilli, *Grace, Faith, Freewill,* 158.

[154] Ibid., 156.

him. It must not be imagined, however, that this "drawing" is a mere influence which may be wholesome and beneficial if followed, but is not always successful.[155]

Again, there are parallels to this text in John 8:47 ("He who is of God hears the words of God") and 10:27 ("My sheep hear My voice, and I know them, and they follow Me").

The critical and debated issue focuses on the effectiveness of God's drawing, speaking, and teaching ministry. Verse 45 clearly states that all who hear and learn from the Father come to Christ; hearing and learning are not mere enabling that falls short of coming to Christ. In theological terms, verse 45 teaches what is often referred to as God's effectual call to salvation. Grudem defines the effectual call as "an act of God the Father, speaking through the human proclamation of the gospel, in which he summons people to himself in such a way that they respond in saving faith."[156]

This truth clearly establishes God's sovereignty in the gift of salvation. While all are invited to come to Christ, only those given to the Son experience this inward work that not only enables them to do so, but actually results in their doing so. Because the Father has given them, they come (v. 37); because they have heard and learned from the Father, they come (v. 45).

This same truth is found in the Apostle Paul's instruction in 1 Corinthians 1:22–24 about the preaching of the gospel:

> For indeed Jews ask for signs and Greeks search for wisdom; but we preach Christ crucified, to Jews a stumbling block and to Gentiles foolishness, but to those who are the called, both Jews and Greeks, Christ the power of God and the wisdom of God.

---

[155] Homer A. Kent, Jr., *Light in the Darkness: Studies in the Gospel of John* (Grand Rapids: Baker, 1974), 107.
[156] *Systematic Theology*, 693.

If the message of Christ crucified is a stumbling block to the Jews and foolishness to the Gentiles, how is that any of them come to believe it? Paul's answer is that some of those who hear the message are "the called" (v. 24). It is obvious that the idea of "called" here does not mean invited; everyone who hears the gospel is invited. Merely being invited does not change the heart from viewing the message as a stumbling block or foolishness. To be "called" in the sense in which this verse uses it is something which effectively transforms the heart so that the same message, Christ crucified, is now viewed as "the power of God and the wisdom of God."

> From any merely human perspective the central message of the Christian gospel must always appear as folly. But to people from both groups this folly turns out to be the very place where God is powerfully at work, calling out a people for his name. Those who are "being saved" (v. 18), the "believing ones" (v. 21), are so because of God's prior action; they are "those whom God has called".... For them the preaching of "Christ crucified" is effectual....[157]

What the Apostle Paul refers to as being "the called" is another way of saying that they have "heard and learned from the Father."

Although this truth is often attacked as destroying man's freedom, this is a misunderstanding of the concept. No one is forced or coerced into salvation. Rather, God graciously illumines the mind so that a true understanding of the gospel takes hold, and, having seen the glory of God in the face of Jesus Christ, the heart turns to Him in saving faith (cf. 2 Cor. 4:4–6). What this truth does demand is the recognition that salvation "does not depend on the man who wills or the man who runs, but on God who has mercy" (Rom. 9:16). In Carson's words, "genuine coming to faith is never finally a matter of autonomous human decision."[158]

---

[157] Gordon D. Fee, *The First Epistle to the Corinthians*, NICNT (Grand Rapids: Eerdmans, 1987), 76–77.

[158] *The Gospel According to John*, 302–3.

## God's Sovereignty in Keeping Them Eternally

The final aspect of God's sovereignty to be considered in relation to salvation is the matter of His preservation of genuine believers. The Lord Jesus Christ also taught that those given to Him by the Father will never be lost: "This is the will of Him who sent Me, that of all that He has given Me I lose nothing, but raise it up on the last day. For this is the will of My Father, that everyone who beholds the Son and believes in Him will have eternal life, and I Myself will raise him up on the last day" (John 6:39–40). The certainty of their eternal salvation is presented from both negative ("I lose nothing") and positive ("I Myself will raise him up") perspectives. The language leaves no room for exceptions: "all that He has given Me."

### *Summary*

Some views of God's sovereignty would never be accused of interfering with the believer's responsibility for evangelism and missions. This attack is usually reserved for those who believe that God's power is exercised with sovereignty over all things, and that God's grace is likewise bestowed according to His sovereign good pleasure. The tension cannot be felt properly without clarity about the extent of God's sovereign control. It is my contention that: 1) God has eternally planned all things which come to pass; 2) God, before the world was created, chose some to salvation; 3) man is unable to respond in repentance and faith without an enabling work of God's grace; 4) God only enables to come to Christ those whom He has given to His Son; 5) when God does draw sinners to Christ, He does so effectually; and 6) none of those who come to Christ will ever be lost, but will all be raised up on the last day.

# *An Apology Regarding God's Sovereignty in Relation to Evangelism and Missions*

Those who reject the understanding of God's sovereignty outlined above often do so by challenging its practical ramifications. They argue that these beliefs destroy our motivation for evangelism and undercut God's program of reaching the lost with the gospel. While it must be conceded that some who believe these doctrines have failed to obey the command of God regarding evangelism, this is an indictment only of those individuals, not necessarily the doctrines themselves. Others who have held these beliefs have been urgent about evangelism and missions. Indeed, some who have rejected these doctrines have been cold and indifferent about evangelism and missions.

But since the charge is made so often, it should be answered. The refutation of this charge is found first in the answer to the question, "What are the biblical motivations for evangelistic zeal and missionary motivation?" Once we have identified these motivations, then we must ask a follow-up question, "Is anything inherent in the doctrine of God's sovereignty outlined above that diminishes these motivations?"

## God's Sovereignty and Our Evangelistic Responsibility

The proper starting place for a biblical understanding of our motivation for evangelism and missions is found in God's command(s) to engage in both.

### A Clearly Given Responsibility
God's people have been given a responsibility and have been commanded to carry out the Great Commission. That forms the bedrock of our motivation because it exalts God to first place in our lives, that is, we live for Him and demonstrate our love for Him through obedience (John 14:15).

In 2 Corinthians 5:17–20, the apostle Paul sets forth the case that those who have been reconciled *to* God have received *from* God a ministry of reconciliation. Notice carefully the argument that he makes in these verses:

> Therefore if anyone is in Christ, he is a new creature; the old things passed away; behold, new things have come. Now all these things are from God, who reconciled us to Himself through Christ and gave us the ministry of reconciliation, namely, that God was in Christ reconciling the world to Himself, not counting their trespasses against them, and He

has committed to us the word of reconciliation. Therefore, we are ambassadors for Christ, as though God were making an appeal through us; we beg you on behalf of Christ, be reconciled to God.

Some might be inclined to see "the ministry of reconciliation" (v. 18) as given only to the apostles, but the context seems to indicate differently.[159] Verse 18 presents the scope of reconciliation provided ("who reconciled us to Himself") as parallel to those who have received the ministry of reconciliation ("gave us the ministry of reconciliation"). The verse which precedes (v. 17) indicates that this ministry grows out of being new creations in Christ, and that is true of "anyone [who] is in Christ."

Also, Paul has already expanded his discussion of his own ministry to include all believers. The accountability he sets forth in vv. 10–11 is presented as being for all believers. It is based on that accountability that he persuades men, and the nature of this persuasion is clearly developed in the verses that follow. The kind of persuasion to which Paul is referring is clearly stated in v. 20: "Therefore, we are ambassadors for Christ, as though God were making an appeal through us; we beg you on behalf of Christ, be reconciled to God." Every believer is called to be an ambassador for Jesus Christ, urging the world to be reconciled to God.

## A Clearly Revealed Accountability

In addition to the more general command to engage in evangelism, the Scriptures indicate that believers are accountable for witnessing to those with whom they have contact. In Acts 20:26 the Apostle Paul declares, "Therefore, I testify to you this day that I am innocent of the blood of all men." The same idea is present in Acts 18:6: "But when they resisted and blasphemed, he shook out his garments and said to them, 'Your blood be on your own heads! I am clean. From now on I will go to the Gentiles.'"

---

[159] For a contrary view, see Paul Barnett, *The Second Epistle to the Corinthians*, NICNT (Grand Rapids: Eerdmans, 1997), 304–5.

It seems that the truth of this text is either abused by those who deny God's sovereignty in salvation or ignored by those who affirm it. That it applies to this discussion can be seen in how commentators have approached it:

> I am not to be charged with the guilt of your condemnation, as owing to my unfaithfulness. This does not mean that he set up a claim to absolute perfection; but that, in the matter under consideration, he had a conscience void of offense.... The word *blood* is used often in the sense of *death*, of blood *shed;* and hence of the guilt or crime of putting one to death.... It here means that if they should die the second death; if they should be lost for ever, *he* would not be to blame. He had discharged his duty in faithful warning and teaching them; and now, if they were lost, the fault would be their own, not his.[160]

> Like the trustworthy watchman in Ezek. 33:1–6, he had sounded the trumpet aloud so that all the province of Asia had heard: if there were any who paid no heed, their blood would be upon their own heads; Paul was free of responsibility for their doom.[161]

> He emphasizes that he has done his part faithfully, so that if anybody falls away, he will not be to blame. He boldly claims that no man's *blood* can be laid on him; for the metaphor see Ezek. 18:13; 33:1–6. The language of guilt for causing a person's death is here applied to the spiritual responsibility of the pastor for faithful presentation of the message that brings life. As the watchman who warns people faithfully of the coming of an enemy is not guilty if they choose to ignore the warning, so it was with Paul as a preacher of the gospel.[162]

---

[160] Albert Barnes, *Acts of the Apostles* (Grand Rapids: Baker, 1953), 294–95.

[161] F. F. Bruce, *The Book of the Acts*, NICNT (Grand Rapids: Eerdmans, 1954), 415.

[162] I. Howard. Marshall, *Acts*, TNTC (Downers Grove, IL: InterVarsity, 1980), 333.

> This plainly refers to that of the prophet (Ezek. 33:6), where the blood of him that perishes by the sword of the enemy is said to be required at the hand of the unfaithful watchman that did not give warning: "You cannot say but I have given warning, and therefore no man's blood can be laid at my door." If a minister has approved himself faithful, he may have this rejoicing in himself, *I am pure from the blood of all men*, and ought to have this testimony from others…. He therefore leaves the blood of those that perish upon their own heads, because they had fair warning given them, but they would not take it.[163]

While there is no basis in this text for excusing the lost from their own ultimate responsibility (e.g., "they would not be lost if you had told them"), it is also not legitimate to avoid the clear implication that believers will be held accountable for their failure to communicate the gospel.

All who stand condemned before God will be so because of their own rejection of His grace and refusal to worship Him (Rom. 1:19–21; Acts 14:17). There will be no excuses for this. However, God's people will also be examined for their service to Christ, including their witness (2 Cor. 5:10). Regarding this judgment, to be "innocent of the blood of all men" means that this responsibility has been completely fulfilled—no one to whom Paul should have declared the gospel had been neglected.

In answer to those who claim that belief in God's sovereign plan for salvation destroys motivation for evangelism and missions, it must be asked, "Does anything about God's sovereignty diminish or eliminate *our obligation* to engage in evangelism actively and to be fervently committed to the Great Commission?" The answer is plainly no.

---

[163] Matthew Henry, *Acts to Revelation* (McLean, VA: MacDonald, n.d.), 265–66.

## God's Sovereignty and Our Evangelistic Desires

A second factor in evangelistic and missionary motivation focuses on the internal desire of believers. In addition to the biblical reality that believers *must* be involved in evangelism and missions, a heart that has been transformed by God's grace will *want* to be involved (Phil. 2:13). Specifically, a growing believer will have desires both for God to be glorified through the gospel and for sinners to be rescued from condemnation.

### A Godward Desire: The Pursuit of His Glory

Conversion radically turns the sinner from being an idol-worshipper into a servant of the true and living God (1 Thess. 1:9). The false glory of dead idols is replaced by the true glory of the living God. The pursuit of this glory becomes the controlling center of life. It is not surprising, then, that Paul, in addressing how believers should relate to unbelievers, establishes the principle that "whatever you do, do all to the glory of God" (1 Cor. 10:31).

### *A Desire for God's Glory to Be Proclaimed*

In 2 Corinthians 4:3–6 Paul confronts the reality that many do not accept the gospel message. In context, he is making it clear that this rejection is not due to any flaws in the message or even in the messengers. If it is rejected, it is because the god of this world has blinded the minds of the unbelieving.

What is particularly important for our consideration is what the devil blinds the lost from seeing. Verse 4 says Satan "has blinded the minds of the unbelieving so that they might not see the light of the gospel of the glory of Christ, who is the image of God." So the devil keeps people trapped in condemnation by blocking their vision of the "glory of Christ, who is the image of God." The heart of the gospel message, therefore, is the glory of Christ. Verse 6 further expands on God's glory in the gospel by describing the gospel message as "the knowledge of the glory of God in the face of Christ." The gospel that saves people is a gospel that reveals God's glory in Jesus Christ. If people don't accept the gospel, it is because they don't see God's glory in it.

This truth is reinforced by the verse that comes between these two phrases. It is precisely because the gospel is "the gospel of the glory of Christ" and "the knowledge of the glory of God in the face of Christ" that Paul without hesitation claims, "we do not preach ourselves but Christ Jesus as Lord." Contrary to many contemporary approaches to evangelism that tailor-make the gospel to fit the needs of the hearer, the biblical gospel focuses first on Christ, not the sinner. We preach Christ, not an eternal life insurance policy or keys to changing your life.

The driving impulse of evangelism and missions, then, is derived from the very message of the gospel, namely that God's glory is revealed in Jesus Christ. Because they have accepted the truth of this message, in a very real sense, believers "cannot stop speaking about what [they] have seen and heard" (Acts 4:20).

### *A Desire for God's Glory to Be Displayed*
Growing out of Paul's unapologetic confession that he is not sufficient for the task he has been given (2 Cor. 2:14–17), but that God is sufficient (2 Cor. 3:5–6), Paul reveals where his hope of "success" in the gospel ministry lies—the power and work of the Holy Spirit (2 Cor. 3:7–11):

> But if the ministry of death, in letters engraved on stones, came with glory, so that the sons of Israel could not look intently at the face of Moses because of the glory of his face, fading as it was, how will the ministry of the Spirit fail to be even more with glory? For if the ministry of condemnation has glory, much more does the ministry of righteousness abound in glory. For indeed what had glory, in this case has no glory because of the glory that surpasses it. For if that which fades away was with glory, much more that which remains is in glory.

The chief term that Paul uses to contrast the ministry of the law and that of the Spirit is *glory*. Central to this is the statement of verse 8: "How will the ministry of the Spirit fail to be even more with *glory*?" How is the ministry of the Spirit more glorious than the old covenant? Because the Spirit's ministry has the power to give life to those under its administration, and that life-giving power is God's power, so God receives the glory.

The fact that lost people are not only dead in trespasses and sins (Eph. 2:1), but actually hostile toward God (Rom. 8:7), makes this powerful work of the Spirit absolutely necessary. Likewise, since the "natural man does not accept the things of the Spirit of God, for they are foolishness to him; and he cannot understand them" (1 Cor. 2:14), the Spirit must illumine the mind before the gospel will ever be understood and accepted. In the language of 2 Corinthians 3, the Spirit must remove the veil that "lies over their heart" (v. 15).

All watered-down views of depravity produce a weakened view of God's saving grace and diminish the glory of the Spirit's work in bringing lost people to faith in Jesus Christ. Repentance and faith are God's gifts produced in hearts by the work of the Spirit (2 Tim. 2:25; Phil. 1:29; 2 Cor. 3:14–18). Songwriter Daniel Whittle expressed the truth beautifully in "I Know Whom I Have Believed":

> I know not how this saving faith
> To me He did impart,
> Nor how believing in His Word,
> Wrought peace within my heart.
> I know not how the Spirit moves,
> Convincing men of sin,
> Revealing Jesus through the Word,
> Creating faith in Him.

This work can only be accomplished by the Spirit's power, and the display of that power brings glory to God (cf. 2 Cor. 4:7). Those who love God and relish His glory also long to see it displayed in the powerful work of the Spirit creating faith in Jesus Christ.

### A Desire for God's Glory to Be Worshipped

As we saw in chapter 1, Paul always roots his missionary efforts in God's glory: "For all things are for your sakes, so that the grace which is spreading to more and more people may cause the giving of thanks to abound to the glory of God" (2 Cor. 4:15). Paul was motivated by the truth that as more people trusted Christ, more praise and worship would ascend to God. The ultimate goal and driving purpose of his evangelism and missionary work was God's glory.

### Summary

A growing believer longs to proclaim God's glory in the face of Jesus Christ, to see God's glory displayed in the power of the Spirit converting sinners, and to see more and more people give God glory through thanksgiving. The product of these God-honoring desires is zeal to declare the gospel to people who are near and to take it those who are far off.

## A Manward Desire: The Rescue of Sinners

When asked what the Great Commandment was, the Lord Jesus replied that it was to "love the Lord your God with all your heart, and with all your soul, and with all your mind" (Matt. 22:37). To this He quickly added the second, "You shall love your neighbor as yourself" (Matt. 22:39). The Lord's parable of the Good Samaritan was given as an exposition of this truth. Confronted with the question, "Who is my neighbor" (Luke 10:29), the Lord told a story which concluded with the question, "Which one of these three do you think proved to be a neighbor to the man who fell into the robbers' hands?" (v. 36). The Lord used this parable to expand the command to love one's neighbor far beyond the narrow scope envisioned by his questioner. By using the Samaritan as his central character and turning the question around ("whose neighbor am I?" versus "who is my neighbor?"), the Lord establishes the principle that genuine love for one's neighbor cannot be applied selectively. We should be a neighbor to all who are in need of help, regardless of "who or what that person may be."[164]

Obedience to this second command demands that believers desire the salvation of the lost—desiring for your neighbor what you desire for yourself must include his or her salvation. A lack of desire for the lost to be saved is both inhuman and ungodly.

---

[164] Norval Geldenhuys, *Commentary on the Gospel of Luke*, NICNT (Grand Rapids: Eerdmans, 1983), 312.

### *It Is Inhuman to Neglect the Salvation of the Lost*

The Lord Jesus Christ set a pattern for us of how we ought to respond to the lost condition of humanity (Matt. 9:36–38; cf. 23:37). Since He is the perfect example of human life in obedience to God's will and conformity to God's character, this pattern established what every human ought to be like. A human heart which is void of compassion at the condition of the lost reveals the sad and hardening effects of the Fall, not the image of God.

The Apostle Paul not only expressed his heart's desire for the salvation of lost people (Rom. 10:1), but he also conducted his ministry in a way that demonstrated the sincerity of that statement through profound sacrifice and enormous exertion (2 Cor. 4:15; 1 Thess. 2:8; Acts 20:31, cf. 2 Cor. 2:4). That this kind of life is expected of all believers is proven from Paul's command to be "imitators of me, just as I also am of Christ" (1 Cor. 11:1). Paul took the pattern of Jesus Christ as normative, and he calls all believers to follow him in following it.

Further, believers have biblical responsibilities to love all people (1 Thess. 3:12) and to do good to all men (Gal 6:10), one implication of which means that we would seek their greatest good—salvation. To be careless or negligent about the eternal welfare of others is inconsistent with, even contradictory to, manifesting biblical love toward them.

### *It Is Ungodly to Neglect the Salvation of the Lost*

Also implicit in the pattern of Jesus Christ is the truth that genuine godliness demands compassion toward the lost and efforts to reach them with the gospel. It is obvious that disobedience regarding the Great Commission is ungodliness. But the ungodliness of neglecting the salvation of the lost runs deeper than the issue of obedience or disobedience. The essence of godliness means reflecting the character of God, and that means that we should respond to the lost in a way that reflects the character of God.

The Bible is clear that God does not take pleasure in the death of the wicked (Ezek. 18:23; 33:11). 1 Timothy 2:4 also states clearly that God "desires all men to be saved and to come to the knowledge of the truth." Although some would take the meaning of "all men" to be "all kinds of men" (i.e., all men without distinction versus all men without exception),[165] such an interpretation is not the only view which is consistent with a strong position regarding divine election to personal salvation. A better approach, it seems, is to recognize in this text a genuine desire on God's part to save, but also to acknowledge, based on the other evidence of Scripture, that God does not determine to fulfill that desire regarding all men.[166] In other words, God desires that all men be saved, yet does not effect their salvation via a display of sovereign grace. Those who deny God's sovereignty over personal salvation find this view unacceptable,[167] but it does have the advantage of harmonizing both types of biblical texts without denying either. Paul is comfortable declaring both that God "desires all men to be saved and to come to the knowledge of the truth" *and* "perhaps God may grant them repentance leading to the knowledge of the truth" (1 Tim 2:4; 2 Tim 2:25). If there are no limits on God's desire, then the word "perhaps" seems out of place. So, if one takes the position that God genuinely desires the salvation of all men, it seems certain that since believers are to reflect the character of God, they should be earnest about desiring the salvation of the lost. To be careless regarding the impending doom of the lost is contrary to the character of God.

These factors all lead to another important question that confronts those who argue that belief in God's sovereignty over salvation destroys evangelistic and missionary motivation: "Is there anything about God's sovereignty that diminishes or eliminates our desire for God to be glorified in saving sinners and for sinners to be rescued from God's wrath?" The answer, again, is a resounding, "No."

---

[165] E.g., George W. Knight III, *The Pastoral Epistles*, NIGTC (Grand Rapids: Eerdmans, 1992), 119.

[166] For a thorough presentation of this view, see John Piper, "Are There Two Wills in God?" in *Still Sovereign*, ed. Thomas R. Schreiner and Bruce A. Ware (Grand Rapids: Baker, 2000), 107–31.

[167] E.g., I. Howard Marshall, *The Pastoral Epistles*, ICC (Edinburgh: T & T Clark, 1999), 427.

## *God's Sovereignty and God's Evangelistic Program*

Another facet of this discussion focuses on how God's eternal plan to bring His chosen ones to salvation will be brought to completion. A central plank in the argument that belief in God's sovereignty over salvation destroys evangelistic and missionary motivation is that such a belief renders evangelism and missions unnecessary. In other words, it is argued that if God has chosen some to salvation and it is certain that they will be saved, then there is no need to witness or take the gospel to them. But this argument misses the mark simply because it ignores the fact that the Scriptures teach that God's sovereign purposes are carried out through, not without, the preaching of the gospel.

### The Reality of God's Program

Romans 10:13–17 is unmistakably clear about the essential nature of gospel preaching:

> For "whoever will call on the name of the Lord will be saved." How then will they call on Him in whom they have not believed? How will they believe in Him whom they have not heard? And how will they hear without a preacher? How will they preach unless they are sent? Just as it is written, "how beautiful are the feet of those who bring good news of good things!" However, they did not all heed the good news; for Isaiah says, "Lord, who has believed our report?" So faith comes from hearing, and hearing by the word of Christ.

The logic of Paul's argument has profound implications regarding both the destiny of the un-evangelized and the responsibility of believers to proclaim the gospel. Only those who have heard the message can believe, and they will only hear if someone takes the message to them. John Piper effectively draws out the implications of this for those who have never heard the gospel:

> Each succeeding question rules out an argument from those who say that there can be salvation without hearing the gospel of Jesus. First, "How are men to call upon him whom they have not believed?" shows that effective calling

presupposes faith in the one called. This rules out the argument that one might call on God savingly without faith in Christ. Second, "And how are they to believe in him whom they have never heard?" shows that faith presupposes hearing Christ in the message of the gospel. This rules out the argument that a person might have saving faith without really knowing or meeting Christ in the gospel. Third, "And how are they to hear without a preacher?" shows that hearing Christ in the gospel presupposes a proclaimer of the gospel. This rules out the argument that one might somehow meet Christ or hear Christ without a messenger to tell the gospel.[168]

It is clear from this text that any claim that God will save apart from the gospel is contrary to the Scriptures. Schreiner supports this conclusion by tying this passage to Paul's earlier instruction in Romans 1:

We have already seen that Paul does not contemplate the possibility that people will be saved by responding positively to natural revelation (see the exegesis and exposition of 1:18–32). All people without exception reject the revelation of God heralded in nature and turn to idolatry. Romans 10:14–17 verifies this interpretation, for it excludes the idea that salvation can be obtained apart from the external hearing of the gospel. Those who call on the Lord in a saving way must believe in him, but this belief is not possible apart from the *hearing* of a message that someone preaches…. When one combines 1:18–32 and 10:14–17, it seems fair to conclude that people are not saved apart from the preaching of the gospel. It is this conviction that has driven the missionary impulse throughout history.[169]

And it is precisely because of this truth that the argument under consideration needs to be turned completely around. Belief in God's sovereign choice of some to salvation does not eliminate the need for

---

[168] *Let the Nations Be Glad!* 155.

[169] Thomas Schreiner, *Romans*, BECNT (Grand Rapids: Baker, 1998), 567–68.

or urgency of evangelism; it actually increases both. Kuiper effectively draws this out:

> Occasionally it is suggested that election makes evangelism superfluous. The question is asked: "If the decree of election is unchangeable and therefore renders the salvation of the elect completely certain, what need have they of the gospel? Will not the elect be saved whether or not they hear the gospel?" The premise of that argumentation is altogether true. Divine election makes the salvation of the elect unalterably certain. But the conclusion drawn from the premise reveals a serious misunderstanding of the divine sovereignty as expressed in the decree of election. While election is from everlasting, the truth may not be lost out of sight that its realization is a process in time. In that process numerous factors play a part. One of those factors is the evangel. And it is a most significant factor.... A most significant conclusion is now warranted. Instead of rendering evangelism superfluous, *election demands evangelism*. All of God's elect must be saved. Not one of them may perish. And the gospel is the means by which God bestows saving faith upon them. In fact, it is the only means which God employs to that end.[170]

The divinely ordained program for calling out a people for His name's sake is the preaching of the gospel, and the reality of both its necessity and success compels participation in it. In fact, one outcome of God's gracious choice of believers to salvation is so they "may proclaim the excellencies of Him who has called [them] out of darkness into His marvelous light" (1 Pet. 2:9).

## The Reason for God's Program
Gospel preaching is a necessary part of God's program for calling in His chosen ones because God's eternal plan encompasses both His goals and the means to accomplish them. "The absolute and unconditional plan of God also incorporates the *means* to the desired

---

[170] R. B. Kuiper, *God-Centered Evangelism* (Carlisle, PA: Banner of Truth, 1966), 37–39.

ends, the causes as well as the effects. Whatever conditions, causes, or other factors are necessary to fulfill the decreed event are themselves decreed. Both ends and means, or purposes and strategies, are comprehended in the decree."[171]

2 Thessalonians 2:13–14 provides a clear biblical framework for understanding the relationship between divinely appointed ends and means:

> But we should always give thanks to God for you, brethren beloved by the Lord, because God has chosen you from the beginning for salvation through sanctification by the Spirit and faith in the truth. It was for this He called you through our gospel, that you may gain the glory of our Lord Jesus Christ.

God's choice of these believers (the divinely-ordained end) was brought to fruition through the preaching of the gospel (the divinely-ordained means). Martin clarifies the connection well:

> God's choice (*eilato*, v. 13) of the Thessalonians differs from his call (*ekalesen*) in v. 14 in that the former is a timeless event within the mind of God. The call, on the other hand, refers to the temporal event at which the apostle proclaimed the gospel, and the Thessalonians had the opportunity to respond to it (cf. Rom 10:14). There could be no ambiguity regarding the avenue by which the Thessalonians heard the call of God. They heard it through the gospel of the Lord Jesus (1:8) preached by Paul and his coworkers (cf. 1 Thess. 1:5).[172]

Packer is also helpful here:

---

[171] Rolland D. McCune, "Systematic Theology I" (class notes, Detroit Baptist Theological Seminary, 1998), 192.

[172] D. Michael Martin, *1, 2 Thessalonians*, NAC (Nashville, TN: Broadman & Holman, 1995), 254.

The appointed *end* cannot be attained apart from the ordained *means*. God accomplishes His saving purposes through, not apart from, gospel preaching. This truth ought to be incentive toward aggressive evangelism because it stresses the crucial role that believers play in God's sovereign purpose to save. "We must realize, therefore, that when God sends us to evangelize, He sends us to act as vital links in the chain of His purpose for the salvation of His elect."[173]

It should also be clear that the responsibility of believers lies in the arena of *means*, not *ends*. God's sovereign plans cannot be used as an excuse for irresponsible, disobedient behavior. William Carey, in expressing the principles that would govern the mission work in India, captured the balance well:

> We are sure that only those who are ordained to eternal life will believe, and that God alone can add to the church such as should be saved. Nevertheless we cannot but observe with admiration that Paul, the great champion for the glorious doctrines of free and sovereign grace, was the most conspicuous for his personal zeal in the work of persuading men to be reconciled to God.[174]

So, in light of the accusation often made that belief in God's sovereignty is detrimental to evangelism and mission, it must be asked, "Is there anything about God's sovereignty that diminishes or eliminates the necessity of evangelism and missions?" Again, the answer is clearly, "No."

### *Summary*

There is nothing about God's sovereignty over all things and over the gift of salvation that undercuts evangelistic and missionary motivation. The believer is obligated to obey God's commands

---

[173] J. I. Packer, *Evangelism and the Sovereignty of God* (Downers Grove, IL: InterVarsity, 1961). 98.

[174] Quoted by Iain H. Murray in *The Puritan Hope* (Carlisle, PA: Banner of Truth, 1971), 145.

regarding evangelism and missions. A growing believer will long to see God glorified and sinners converted by His grace. God's sovereign plan includes both the ends and the means to those ends, so evangelism and missionary activity are necessary. Or, to look at it from another perspective, evangelism and missions are both *important* (because of the believer's obligations and desires) and *urgent* (because of their necessity). This combination of the importance and urgency fuels the believer's motivation for evangelism and missions.

## A Polemic Regarding God's Sovereignty in Relation to Evangelism and Missions

The purpose here is to turn the tables, so to speak, in this discussion. Rather than being detrimental to evangelism and missions, a settled conviction about God's sovereignty over all things, including the gift of salvation, is a powerful stimulus for the work of evangelism and missions. This stimulus is found in the benefits of believing both that God is sovereign in His rule over all things and in His granting of salvation.

### The Benefits of Believing that God is Sovereign Over All Things

Acknowledging the biblical teaching regarding God's comprehensive control over all things produces confidence in believers as they face a wide range of challenges.

**Confidence That God Can Answer Prayer**
This belief produces confidence that God can answer important prayer requests that affect the success of our witness and missionary endeavors. Specifically, God's sovereign power enables Him 1) to move the wills of His people so that they go into the harvest (Matt. 9:37–38; cf. Rom. 10:15); 2) to protect His servants as they serve Him in the gospel (2 Thess. 3:2; Rom. 15:30–32); and 3) to cause the Word to spread rapidly and be glorified (2 Thess. 3:1).

While those who deny God's complete sovereignty over all things would no doubt claim to pray confidently about these matters, retaining the concept of autonomous freewill removes the ground for confidence—God is certainly limited in what He can do in answer to each of these requests. He can work externally to move and position people, but He cannot effectively change the heart and will.[175] The net result is that the Great Commission is ultimately contingent on the decision of human will, and God cannot change that. Thankfully, the biblical portrait of God's sovereignty stands in stark contrast to this weak picture of divine power and control. As Bingham Hunter notes, "To be worth praying to, God has first of all got to have the power to do what we ask. Second, he must have the sovereignty over creation to do what he wants to do."[176]

## Confidence That God Can Control the Direction and Destiny of Nations

God's sovereignty over all things is the basis of missionary confidence that He can control the direction and destiny of nations, whether ruled by believers or pagans. Consider some biblical illustrations of this grand truth:

- And they observed the Feast of Unleavened Bread seven days with joy, for the Lord had caused them to rejoice, and had turned the heart of the king of Assyria toward them to encourage them in the work of the house of God, the God of Israel (Ezra 6:22).
- Blessed be the Lord, the God of our fathers, who has put such a thing as this in the king's heart, to adorn the house of the Lord which is in Jerusalem (Ezra 7:27).
- The king's heart is like channels of water in the hand of the Lord; He turns it wherever He wishes (Prov. 21:1).
- But Sihon king of Heshbon was not willing for us to pass through his land; for the Lord your God hardened his spirit and made his heart obstinate, in order to deliver him into your hand, as he is today (Deut. 2:30).

---

[175] E.g., Dick Eastman, *The Hour That Changes the World* (Grand Rapids: Baker, 1978), 158.

[176] *The God Who Hears* (Downers Grove, IL: Inter Varsity, 1986), 48.

Why were believers able to turn to God in fervent prayer to tear down the Iron Curtain? It is because the Scriptures are clear that God is fully able to accomplish that which they ask. If He can use a pagan king to send His people back to the Promised Land, then He can turn the heart of the Communist Chinese leaders. On the other hand, those who argue vehemently for libertarian freewill build a wall around the "king's heart" that prevents God from turning it "wherever He wishes."

## Confidence That God Can Overcome All Opposition to His Purposes

God's irresistible power is the source of confidence that He can overcome all obstacles to the fulfillment of His purposes. In this case, irresistible does not mean that it cannot be resisted, but that it cannot be resisted successfully. Again, consider the biblical portrait of this irresistible power:

- All the inhabitants of the earth are accounted as nothing, But He does according to His will in the host of heaven And among the inhabitants of earth; And no one can ward off His hand Or say to Him, 'What have You done?' (Dan. 4:35).
- I know that You can do all things, And that no purpose of Yours can be thwarted (Job 42:2).
- But our God is in the heavens; He does whatever He pleases (Ps. 115:3).
- Whatever the Lord pleases, He does, In heaven and in earth, in the seas and in all deeps (Ps. 135:6).

Whatever God purposes to do, He can accomplish, and no one can stand in His way. This was the confidence that sustained William Carey through his years of struggle and suffering for the sake of the gospel:

> When I left England, my hope of India's conversion was very strong; but amongst so many obstacles, it would die, unless upheld by God. Well, I have God, and His Word is true. Though the superstitions of the heathen were a thousand times stronger than they are, and the example of the Europeans a thousand times worse; though I were deserted

by all and persecuted by all, yet my faith, fixed on that sure Word, would rise above all obstructions and overcome every trial. God's cause will triumph.[177]

Those who reject God's complete sovereignty would claim to agree with Carey, but the sad consequence of exalting man's will to the place of virtual co-sovereign is that it destroys our confidence in the power of God to accomplish His purposes regardless of opposition.

## Confidence That God Can Cause All Things to Work for Good

God's sovereign control over all things is the root of the believer's confidence that God can actively superintend all the details of life for His glory and His children's good. Sadly, the contemporary desire to squeeze God into a more relational mold actually reduces Him to a player alongside of humanity in the cosmic game. And as a player in their scheme, He does not control all things; He responds to the unfolding course of events in a way similar to humans. How can a God like that fulfill the promise of Scripture that He will cause "all things to work together for good to those who love God, to those who are called according to His purpose" (Rom. 8:28)?

Those who deny God's specific sovereignty over all things must weaken the point of this text. John Sanders serves as example of this:

> In my view, God does seek to bring good even out of tragedy, but there are no guarantees.... Considering the personal aspects of the divine-human relationship, though God works to bring good out of evil, God cannot *guarantee* that a greater good will arise out of each and every occurrence of evil.[178]

Given Sanders presupposition, he is correct to arrive at his conclusion. If God cannot control the actions of man, then the truth of this text is suspended on chance, not sovereignty. Thankfully, the Scriptures are clear that Sanders presupposition is incorrect. God can and does work through even the most sinful actions of man to

---

[177] Quoted by Iain H. Murray in *The Puritan Hope*, 140.
[178] *The God Who Risks* (Downers Grove, IL: InterVarsity, 1998), 263.

accomplish His purposes as He did in the life of Joseph and in the crucifixion of His Son. This truth serves as a source of enormous comfort and strength for those who face hardship and persecution for the gospel of Jesus Christ.

## *The Benefits of Believing that God is Sovereign Over Salvation*

Firm conviction regarding the sovereignty of God's saving grace also produces confidence in believers as they engage in the tasks of evangelism and missions.

### Confidence That God Will Open Doors for the Word

The powerful combination of God's purpose in election and the necessity of gospel proclamation produces confidence that God can and will open whatever doors need to be opened in order for the gospel to advance to its appointed end. This is the ground of Paul's request for prayer from the Colossian congregation: "Devote yourselves to prayer, keeping alert in it with an attitude of thanksgiving; praying at the same time for us as well, that God will open up to us a door for the word" (Col. 4:2-3).

### Confidence That God Controls the Harvest

The timing and size of the harvest is under the sovereign control of God. Embracing this truth allows believers to participate faithfully in the harvest according to the role that He assigns, free from man-made pressure to produce that which only God can do. Jesus' interaction with the Samaritan woman and the instruction He gave His disciples informs us that evangelism is a process that involves sowing and reaping. In light of the fast-approaching harvest of Samaritans, Jesus told His disciples, "I sent you to reap that for which you have not labored; others have labored and you have entered into their labor" (John 4:38). Others had been involved in the labor, but were not divinely appointed to be involved in the reaping. But because the harvest is the Lord's, His people are only expected to be faithful for their assigned task. If God assigns the task of sowing, then sowing can be done in confidence that God will complete the harvest in His appointed time.

## Confidence That God Gives Repentance and Faith

The sovereignty of God's grace means that God can work effectively in the hearts of sinners to draw them to Christ (John 6:44–45) by granting them repentance and faith (2 Tim. 2:25–26; Phil. 1:29). Sovereign grace means that God can work within the sinner to turn him from sin to Christ; He is not limited to external influence nor restricted in the amount of influence He can exert. Packer highlights the confidence which the evangelist or missionary can draw from God's sovereignty:

> So far from making evangelism pointless, the sovereignty of God in grace is the one thing that prevents evangelism from being pointless. For it creates the possibility—indeed, the certainty—that evangelism will be fruitful. Apart from it, there is not even a possibility of evangelism being fruitful. Were it not for the sovereign grace of God, evangelism would be the most futile and useless enterprise that the world has ever seen, and there would be no more complete waste of time under the sun than to preach the Christian gospel.[179]

For those who hold other views regarding God's sovereignty, these may seem like excessively strong claims. However, Piper, by turning the tables, drives home the seriousness of this issue:

> People who really believe that man must have the ultimate power of self-determination, can't consistently pray that God would convert the unbelieving sinners. Why? Because if they pray for divine influence in a sinner's life they are either praying for a successful influence (which takes away the sinner's ultimate *self*-determination), or they are praying for an unsuccessful influence (which is not praying for *God* to convert the sinner). So either you give up praying for God to convert sinners or you give up ultimate human self-determination.[180]

---

[179] Packer, *Evangelism & the Sovereignty of God*, 106.

[180] John Piper, *The Pleasures of God* (Portland, OR: Multnomah, 1991), 226.

## Confidence That God Will Call Out a People from the Nations

What is true of individuals, namely that God will save those He has chosen, extends to the ends of the earth. This confidence fuels the missionary enterprise. God told Paul, *prior to* his ministry in Corinth, that He had "many people in [that] city" (Acts 18:10). In a similar way, modern missionaries can follow the Lord's direction into the harvest fields of the world confident about the success of their efforts. The Lord Himself expressed this confidence about the mission of His disciples:

- All that the Father gives Me will come to Me, and the one who comes to Me I will certainly not cast out (John 6:37).
- I have other sheep, which are not of this fold; I must bring them also, and they will hear My voice; and they will become one flock with one shepherd (John 10:16).
- You did not choose Me but I chose you, and appointed you that you would go and bear fruit, and that your fruit would remain, so that whatever you ask of the Father in My name He may give to you (John 15:16).
- I do not ask on behalf of these alone, but for those also who believe in Me through their word (John 17:20).

The note of certainty in these texts should not be missed or minimized. The mission of Jesus Christ is not hanging on a thread of human contingency. The Lord was certain that His sheep would be gathered. What was the source of this confidence?

> Jesus' confidence does not rest in the potential for a positive response among well-meaning people. Far from it: his confidence is in his Father to bring to pass the Father's redemptive purposes: *All that the Father gives me will come to me.* Jesus' confidence in the success of his mission is frankly predestinarian.[181]

Before the Son left Heaven, He knew that His mission was sure to accomplish the objective of bringing in people "from every tribe and

---

[181] Carson, *The Gospel According to John*, 290.

tongue and people and nation" (Rev 5:9). This mission was never threatened in any way by the will of man because it was rooted in the sovereign purposes of God. As His ambassadors, believers ought to live with the same confident expectation that their witness for Christ and missionary endeavors will prosper under the good, all-powerful hand of God.

## *Conclusion*

*Biblically* and *theologically*, there is no basis for eliminating evangelistic and missionary responsibility due to divine sovereignty. If believers choose to do so, they do it against the teaching of the Bible and the godly examples in it, not because of them. Furthermore, there is nothing in these doctrines that should diminish the proper motivations for evangelism and missions. *Practically*, since believers are not sovereign, they must concentrate on the responsibility side of this discussion while trusting God to use their obedience to accomplish His purposes. Evangelism and missions are critically important, so believers must engage in them. And these tasks are urgent, so faithful Christians must be diligent and zealous about them.

# ABOUT THE AUTHOR

**David M. Doran** is the senior pastor of Inter-City Baptist Church and President of Detroit Baptist Theological Seminary. He serves as the Chairman of the Practical Theology Department and teaches the core pastoral theology courses in the M.Div. program. Dr. Doran received a B.A. from Bob Jones University and both the M.Div. and Th.M. from DBTS. He earned his D.Min. from Trinity Evangelical Divinity School. Over several decades at ICBC, Dr. Doran has conducted an effective expository preaching and teaching ministry, established Grace Baptist Mission, and expanded outreach through campus evangelism and discipleship, mission conferences and more.

Made in the USA
Columbia, SC
03 August 2023

21174681R00117